Thai cooking
made easy

Thai cooking
made easy

Discover the exotic tastes of Thailand with
over 60 fabulous step-by-step recipes

Becky Johnson

HERMES
HOUSE

This edition is published by Hermes House
an imprint of Anness Publishing Ltd, Hermes House,
88–89 Blackfriars Road, London SE1 8HA
tel. 020 7401 2077; fax 020 7633 9499
www.hermeshouse.com; www.annesspublishing.com

If you like the images in this book and would like to investigate using
them for publishing, promotions or advertising, please visit our website
www.practicalpictures.com for more information.

Publisher: Joanna Lorenz
Editorial Director: Judith Simons
Editors: Susannah Blake and Elizabeth Woodland
Copy Editor: Jenni Fleetwood
Editorial Readers: Penelope Goodare and Jay Thundercliffe
Photographer: Nicki Dowey
Food Stylist: Lucy McKelvie
Stylist: Helen Trent
Designer: Nigel Partridge
Jacket Designer: Whitelight Design Associates
Production Controller: Wendy Lawson

ETHICAL TRADING POLICY
Because of our ongoing ecological investment programme, you, as our
customer, can have the pleasure and reassurance of knowing that a tree
is being cultivated on your behalf to naturally replace the materials used
to make the book you are holding. For further information about this
scheme, go to www.annesspublishing.com/trees

.Previously published as part of a larger volume *Thai Food and Cooking*

PUBLISHER'S NOTE:
Although the advice and information in this book are believed to be
accurate and true at the time of going to press, neither the authors nor
the publisher can accept any legal responsibility or liability for any
errors or omissions that may be made.

NOTES

Bracketed terms are for American readers.

For all recipes, quantities are given in both metric and
imperial measures and, where appropriate, measures
are also given in standard cups and spoons.
Follow one set, but not a mixture because they
are not interchangeable.

Standard spoon and cup measures are level.
1 tsp = 5ml, 1 tbsp = 15ml, 1 cup = 250ml/8fl oz

Australian standard tablespoons are 20ml.
Australian readers should use 3 tsp in place of 1 tbsp
for measuring small quantities of gelatine,
cornflour, salt etc.

Medium (US large) eggs are used unless
otherwise stated.

CONTENTS

INTRODUCTION

The Thai cuisine is one of the jewels of the East, with its fiery flavours sitting in perfect harmony with subtle, fragrant aromas, sweet, creamy sauces and fresh, crunchy textures, all combined in endless delicious ways.

In the last few years, the popularity of Thai food and cooking has grown enormously. With improved transport and lower air fares, more and more people are visiting Thailand and are able to experience the cuisine at first hand. Restaurants serving excellent, authentic Thai dishes have become commonplace. Classic Thai ingredients such as lemon grass and kaffir lime leaves that were once hard to find and had to be sought out in specialist Asian stores are now available in most large supermarkets – opening up a wealth of possibilities to the home cook.

Another reason for Thai food's growing popularity is that it is perfectly suited to busy, modern lives. The majority of Thai dishes can be cooked quickly and use healthy cooking methods such as grilling (broiling), steaming, stir-frying and braising.

Fresh vegetables, healthy fish and shellfish, tofu and low-fat cuts of meat and poultry are used in savoury dishes, and a variety of desserts are often fruit-based. Vegetables and fruit are usually served raw or lightly cooked so they retain their taste, texture and valuable nutrients.

Not only are dishes quick and healthy, they can often be made using just one pan. The wok, which is the most useful vessel for Thai cooking, is so versatile that it can be used for frying, steaming and simmering. This means that you can use the wok to cook whole dishes, which will save time on washing up after dinner.

THE SECRET OF THE THAI CUISINE

Thai cooking relies on the use of the "five flavours": salty, sweet, sour, bitter and hot. Salty flavourings such as soy sauce, Thai fish sauce, shrimp paste and oyster sauce help to bring out the flavours of the other ingredients. Sweet ingredients such as palm sugar and coconut milk help to enhance the flavour of herbs and spices in savoury

dishes. Sour flavourings such as lime juice, tamarind and rice vinegar help to accentuate other flavours. The bitter taste, which is introduced through the addition of herbs and green vegetables, is balanced against the other four flavours. The main source of heat is chilli – either fresh, dried, in pastes or in sauces – but heat is also introduced through ginger, onions and garlic.

It is the perfect balance of these five elements that gives Thai food its distinctive character. Each recipe in this book utilizes the basic principle of the five flavours to create fabulous, authentic dishes that will transport you to another world.

EATING THAI-STYLE

In Thailand, meals are a time for family and friends to gather together, share food and enjoy. Foods can be separated into savoury and sweet, but within this distinction dishes are usually served together rather than as several separate courses. A traditional Thai meal will usually consist of clear soup served with steamed rice, a steamed or braised dish, a fried dish, a salad and a spicy sauce. The dishes should offer a range of different tastes and textures, creating a perfect harmony of flavours. Fresh fruit is typically served after the meal, but there are also more elaborate sweet dishes based on fruit and coconut that are utterly delicious.

STRESS-FREE SHORTCUTS

If you're in a real hurry, there are plenty of shortcuts for many of the recipes in this book. Spice pastes are traditionally pounded by hand in a mortar but you can cut many minutes of preparation time by whizzing the ingredients together in a food processor. Curry pastes can also be made in advance and stored in an airtight container in the refrigerator until ready to use. (If even this seems like too much effort, you can buy excellent ready-made Thai

Left: You can serve duck curry with plain boiled rice for a simple meal, or as part of a selection of dishes for a delicious Thai feast.

Above: Traditional Thai ingredients, such as curry paste and fish sauce, make for an unusual and delicious vegetable dish.

Above right: These satay sticks served with an aromatic and spicy peanut sauce are very popular and surprisingly easy to make.

pastes in most large supermarkets – so add some jars to the store cupboard.)

When you buy fish or shellfish, ask the fishmonger to clean and prepare it for you so you can just take it home and cook it. After all, no one should have to prepare squid, or fillet a fish, after a long, hard day at work. The same is true when buying meat and poultry. Ask the butcher to prepare cuts of meat to save you time once you get home.

Think about the whole meal before you start preparing ingredients. Decide what you want to eat, then look at the recipes and see how long each one is going to take. If something needs to stand for 10 or 20 minutes – work this into your preparation time. If you're missing a key ingredient, choose a different recipe. If a dessert needs to be chilled for an hour or two, make this first then put it in the refrigerator while you make the rest of the meal. Planning and forethought are the simplest ways to guarantee stress-free, perfect results, and you will also have more time for yourself or to prepare for your guests.

ABOUT THIS BOOK

This book is devoted to helping you enjoy the taste of authentic Thai cooking, even when time is short. Each recipe should take less than 30 minutes to prepare, and they have been grouped into seven chapters so that you can easily pick the right dishes for the occasion. You can choose a selection of dishes to create a traditional-style Thai meal, or just serve a simple meal with one main dish and boiled rice or noodles.

If you are planning a three-course feast, there are a fabulous selection of appetizers to munch on. Some, such as fish cakes, can be prepared in advance so you can save time on the day. You'll find that even some of the snacks that look more difficult, such as samosas, are surprisingly quick and simple to make.

The desserts are straightforward to prepare, too. Cold desserts can be made before the main course and then chilled until ready to serve, while the hot desserts take very little time to make. Fruits, such as pumpkins or bananas, are delicious stewed in coconut milk and are very easy to prepare, while a rich ice cream or a cool and refreshing ice can be made the night before, and enjoyed whenever you like.

Below: Thai desserts are often based on fruit and make a light and refreshing finish to a meal.

THE MAIN INGREDIENTS

Thai cuisine is based on simple, fresh ingredients. Many, such as fresh root ginger, garlic and soy sauce, will be familiar to most Western cooks, but there are other ingredients that may be less well-known. This section looks at all the classic ingredients needed to create authentic Thai food, with tips on buying, preparing and cooking.

ESSENTIAL FLAVOURINGS

The secret of Thai cooking is the judicious use of flavourings – from fresh herbs, spices and aromatics to sour lime juice, sweet palm sugar and fragrant jasmine flowers.

Basil

Three different types of basil are used in Thai cooking: Thai, holy and lemon. Thai basil has a sweet, aniseed flavour and is used in red curries. It is similar in appearance to Western sweet basil, which can be used as a substitute. Holy, or hot, basil has a pungent flavour and is used with fish, poultry and beef. Lemon basil is a small, delicate variety that is rarely found outside Asia. In Thailand, it is used in soups and sprinkled over salads.

Mint

Fresh mint is a popular flavouring in Thai cooking, particularly in salads.

Below: Fresh root ginger is an essential ingredient in Thai cooking, adding a fresh, peppery flavour to many dishes.

Above: Holy basil has dull green leaves and a much stronger flavour than Western sweet basil.

Chives

Long, thin chives have a delicate onion flavour and are often used as a garnish. Chinese, or garlic, chives are bigger than the Western variety and have a much stronger, more garlicky flavour.

Coriander/Cilantro

The whole coriander plant – leaves, roots and seeds – is used in Thai cooking. The fragrant leaves are used in soups, sauces and curries and as a garnish. The fresh herb is very delicate so should be used as soon as possible after purchase. The roots are crushed and used for marinades; they will keep for several days in the refrigerator. The round brown seeds have a warm, aromatic flavour and are used in curry pastes. They can be stored in an airtight container for many months. The ground spice loses its flavour quickly so it is better to buy whole seeds and grind them as and when required.

Ginger

This knobbly root has a papery, brown skin covering the firm, fresh, zesty, peppery flesh. The skin is removed, then the flesh is sliced, chopped or pounded to a paste and used in curries, stir-fries, soups, salads and marinades. It can be stored, wrapped, in the refrigerator for up to 2 weeks.

Galangal

This knobbly rhizome is a member of the ginger family and has a similar appearance. There are two varieties: greater and lesser galangal. The latter is favoured in Thai cooking. Its flavour is a cross between fresh root ginger and black pepper and it is often used in jungle curries and with fish. It is prepared and used in much the same way as fresh root ginger. Fresh galangal is available in Asian stores and can be stored, wrapped, in the refrigerator for up to 2 weeks.

Lemon grass

This slightly woody, pale green stem is an essential Thai flavouring. It is used in savoury dishes and desserts to impart a delicate citrus flavour. The fibrous layers surrounding the stalk are generally removed, then the fleshy bulbous end of the stalk shredded or pounded to a paste. The whole stalk, or just the upper portion, may be lightly bruised with a pestle and used to flavour stocks. Fresh lemon grass stalks are sold in bunches in supermarkets and Asian stores. Dried and bottled chopped lemon grass are a poor substitute for the fresh herb.

Coconut

This large, brown, hairy nut is an essential ingredient in Thai cooking – used both for its flavour and its rich creamy consistency. Coconut milk, cream, shredded fresh coconut and desiccated (dry unsweetened shredded) coconut are used in both sweet and savoury dishes. When choosing fresh coconuts, select nuts that feel heavy; when you shake them you should be able to hear liquid sloshing about inside. Coconut milk and cream are available in cans and cartons; desiccated coconut canes in packets. Blocks of creamed coconut are also sometimes available, and can be grated and reconstituted using a little boiling water.

Above: Fragrant, zesty lemon grass is one of the essential flavours used in both sweet and savoury Thai dishes.

Garlic

This pungent member of the onion family is used extensively in Thai cooking. Thai garlic has a pinkish skin and tends to be more potent than Western varieties. Small bulbs of garlic preserved in sweet and sour brine are also a popular flavouring and condiment and are available from Asian stores. Garlic oil has a pleasant aroma and is used to impart a delicate flavour to dishes; it is available from Asian stores and large supermarkets.

Kaffir lime leaves

These dark green, shiny leaves are an essential flavouring in many Thai dishes. The leaves are usually torn or shredded before adding to a dish to release their distinctive citrus flavour. To shred leaves, cut out the tough stem, then roll the leaf into a tight scroll and slice. The leaves are available in most large supermarkets and Asian stores.

Chillies

Fiery chillies are an essential part of most savoury Thai dishes. Fresh, dried or infused in oil, they are used to add heat and flavour to salads, soups, stir-fries, curries, pickles and sauces. Tiny red and green bird's eye chillies are extremely hot and much favoured in Thai cooking. Long, or cayenne, chillies

are milder than bird's eye ones. They are often used as a garnish, or dried and used in red curry paste. Dried chillies are also widely used – whole or crushed – and may be roasted to heighten their flavour before adding to dishes. Crushed dried chillies are offered as a condiment at the table and sprinkled over food to taste.

Much of the heat of chillies is contained in the seeds and white membranes surrounding the seeds so it is wise to remove these, unless you prefer your dishes fiery-hot. Chillies contain capsaicin, which can cause intense irritation to the skin and eyes, so always wash your hands with soap and water immediately after handling, or wear rubber (latex) gloves when preparing chillies.

Peppercorns

Before chillies were introduced to Thailand in the 16th century, pepper was used to add heat to dishes. Today, white peppercorns, which have a much milder flavour than black, are used for seasoning. Green peppercorns, which are the unripe berries, have a less complex flavour than white, and are used as a garnish for jungle curries and stir-fries. They are available fresh or bottled in brine: bottled ones should be drained and rinsed before use.

Below: Blisteringly hot red and green bird's eye chillies are used to add heat and flavour to many Thai dishes.

Above: Turmeric is a glorious yellow-orange colour but the juice can stain, so handle it with care.

Turmeric

The fresh spice resembles fresh root ginger but has bright orange-yellow flesh. It has a peppery aroma and slightly musky flavour and is often used in curry pastes. The dried spice is the same bright yellow colour and is usually available ground. (The dried root is sometimes available, but it is very hard and difficult to grind.) Fresh turmeric is available from Asian stores and can be stored, wrapped, in the refrigerator for up to 2 weeks.

Cumin

Ground cumin is often used in curry pastes. Once ground, the spice loses its aroma quickly, so it is best to buy whole seeds, then grind them in a mortar or spice grinder as you need them.

Fennel

These small, brown, oval seeds have a slightly aniseedy flavour. They are often used ground in savoury dishes.

Five-spice powder

This classic Chinese spice blend is a mixture of Sichuan peppercorns, cinnamon, cloves, fennel seeds and star anise and has a warm, fragrant aroma. It is very popular in Thailand and goes particularly well with duck, pork and beef.

Tamarind

Commonly used as a souring agent to bring out and enhance the flavour of other ingredients, tamarind has a fruity, sharp taste, not unlike sour dates. Fresh tamarind pods are common in Asia, but you are more likely to find blocks of compressed tamarind or tubs of tamarind paste in the West. To use compressed tamarind, soak about 15ml/1 tbsp in 150ml/¼ pint/⅔ cup warm water for 10 minutes, then stir to release the pulp and strain the juice. Discard the pulp remaining in the sieve (strainer) and stir the juice into the dish. To use tamarind paste, simply mix with a little warm water, then add to the dish.

Limes

Sharp, tangy limes are widely used in Thai dishes and add the essential sour flavour to sweet and savoury dishes. The sourness of the juice brings out the flavours of other ingredients and is used to balance the intense sweetness of many fruits and desserts.

Rice vinegar

Made from fermented rice, this vinegar has a sharp, tangy flavour and is used to add a sour element to many Thai dishes. It is available from Asian stores and large supermarkets.

Below: Palm sugar is usually available in blocks and can vary in colour from pale gold to light brown.

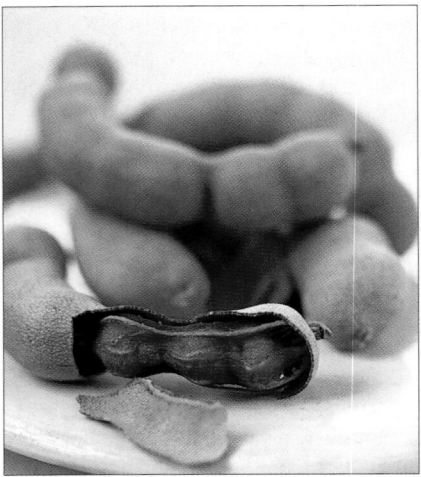

Above: The tart, fruity pulp found inside tamarind pods is used as a souring agent in many Thai dishes.

Sesame oil

This strongly flavoured, nutty, brown oil is used for flavouring rather than cooking. It is generally sprinkled over food just before serving. It is available from supermarkets and Asian stores.

Mekhong whisky

This potent rice whisky is similar to bourbon in flavour. It may be enjoyed as a drink, but is also used as a flavouring in dishes such as jungle curry.

Palm sugar

Also known as jaggery, palm sugar is made from the sap of various palms. It varies from light to deep golden brown, has a crumbly texture and is usually available in blocks. It has a distinctive flavour and is slightly less sweet than cane sugar. To use, grate off as much sugar as you need. If you cannot find palm sugar, soft brown sugar is a fairly good substitute.

Jasmine flowers

These pretty, delicate white flowers have a light, floral fragrance and are often infused in syrup and used to flavour desserts and cakes. The flowers are available only in season. Jasmine essence can be used as a substitute but it lacks the subtlety imparted by the fresh flowers.

SPICE PASTES

There are many classic Thai curry pastes, all with their own individual blends of herbs and spices. Green, red and yellow curry pastes are used to make hot curries with plenty of liquid. Very good ready-made versions are available in most supermarkets.

Green curry paste

This hot and spicy paste is a blend of chillies, aromatics and plenty of fresh herbs, giving the finished paste a greenish colour. It is most often used to make chicken and vegetable curries.

Red curry paste

Made with plenty of fresh red chillies, this fiery, red-brown paste is a complex blend of aromatics and spices. It is most frequently used in beef and chicken curries.

Yellow curry paste

This golden brown paste is very spicy. It contains fresh turmeric and is usually used in chicken and beef curries.

Magic paste

This fragrant paste made from crushed garlic, white pepper and coriander (cilantro) is often used to flavour soups and curries. It is available from Thai and Asian stores.

Below: Good quality yellow curry paste can be bought ready-made from Asian stores and some large supermarkets.

SAUCES

There are a number of essential sauces used for flavouring Thai dishes. Some are also used as a condiment.

Fish sauce

Nam pla is one of the most important ingredients used in the Thai kitchen. Made from fermented salted fish, the clear orange-brown sauce has a very salty, pungent aroma and flavour that mellows during cooking. It is available from Asian stores.

Soy sauce

Two types of soy sauce are used in Thai cooking: salty and sweet. There are light and dark varieties of both salty and sweet sauces. They are most frequently used in stir-fries, sauces and dressings. Soy sauce can vary greatly in quality, so buy a reputable brand. Store it in the refrigerator once opened.

Chilli sauce

This thick, dark red sauce is very fiery and is used for flavouring and as a condiment. Use with caution because it is very strong. It is available from most supermarkets and Asian stores.

Shrimp paste

Also known as blachan or terasi, this dark brown paste is a key flavouring in Thai cooking. Made from fermented, salted and dried pulverized shrimp, it has a very pungent flavour and is usually heated before adding to a dish to help mellow the flavour. It is available from Asian stores in compressed blocks, cans or tubs.

Dried shrimp

These tiny, salty shellfish have a strong flavour and are used as a flavouring in salads and other dishes. They are available in Asian stores, and are usually found in plastic bags in the chiller or freezer cabinets. Choose shrimp with a pinkish colour, and avoid any with a greyish tinge.

Above: Piquant sweet chilli sauce is used both as a flavouring and as a spicy dipping sauce.

Sweet chilli sauce

This thick translucent orange sauce is specked with red chilli. It has a much more delicate, fruitier flavour than chilli sauce and may be used as a flavouring ingredient or dipping sauce. It is available from supermarkets and Asian stores.

Black bean sauce

This pungent mixture of puréed black beans, soy sauce, sugar and spices is used to add an earthy flavour to many savoury dishes. It is available from Asian stores and some supermarkets.

Oyster sauce

This thick, dark brown sauce originated in China but is popular in Thai cooking. Based on soy sauce and oyster extract, it has a distinctive salty, slightly sweet taste and is used as a flavouring in many dishes. It is best added towards the end of cooking time. It is available from Asian stores and supermarkets. A vegetarian version made from mushrooms is also available.

Plum sauce

This tangy, spicy sweet-and-sour sauce also originated in China. It is used as a flavouring ingredient and also as a dipping sauce. It is widely available in large supermarkets and Asian stores.

RICE

In Thailand, rice is considered the most important ingredient: the average Thai consumes about 158kg/350lb rice a year. There are two main types: jasmine (or Thai) fragrant rice and glutinous rice. Jasmine rice has long grains and a scented flavour. Once cooked, the translucent grains become white and fluffy. Glutinous rice, also known as sweet or sticky rice, may have short, round grains or long grains. When cooked, they clump together, allowing the rice to be rolled into balls and eaten with the hands. Rice flour, made from ground rice, is also widely used – in noodles, pancakes and desserts.

Cooking jasmine rice

The amount of water needed will vary slightly depending on variety, but as a general guide, use about 600ml/1 pint/2½ cups water for 225g/8oz/generous 1 cup rice.

1 Put the rice in a large bowl and pour over cold water to cover. Gently swirl the grains until the water turns cloudy. Leave to settle, then drain. Repeat several times until the water runs clear.

2 Put the rice in a pan and pour in the measured water. Bring to the boil, then reduce the heat to very low. Cover tightly and cook until all the liquid has been absorbed (up to 25 minutes).

3 Remove the pan from the heat and leave, covered, in a warm place for 5 minutes until tender.

Above: Fresh egg noodles usually come packed in nests, and are available from Chinese and Asian supermarkets.

NOODLES

Different types of noodles are used either as an ingredient or an accompaniment. Rice noodles are made from rice flour and come in several widths: very thin vermicelli rice noodles, medium rice noodles, which resemble spaghetti, and rice stick noodles, which are flat, rather like tagliatelle. All are available dried; rice stick noodles are also available fresh. Rice noodles do not need to be boiled, they can simply be soaked in boiling water for a few minutes until soft. Fresh noodles are sticky so should be separated before soaking.

Yellow egg noodles are made with wheat flour. They are available fresh or dried and come in various shapes: round ones for stir-frying and flat ones for soups. Egg noodles need to be cooked in boiling water for 4 minutes, or according to the packet instructions.

Transparent cellophane noodles, also known as glass or bean thread noodles, are very thin and wiry. Available dried, they are always used as an ingredient. To prepare, soak in boiling water.

FISH AND SHELLFISH

Thailand has long coastlines and many rivers, which offer an abundant supply of fish and shellfish, including prawns (shrimp), crab, squid, and many types of fish. They are used in many dishes.

POULTRY AND MEAT

Chicken is used in many Thai dishes, including salads, soups, stir-fries and curries. Duck and guinea fowl are also popular. Pork is widely eaten throughout South-east Asia, and beef is also used.

TOFU

Also known as beancurd, tofu is made from fermented soya beans. There are two types of fresh tofu: silken and firm. Silken tofu is very soft and is often used in soups, while firm tofu can withstand more rigorous handling. Both are a creamy white colour, and are sold in blocks. Deep-fried tofu is golden brown and chewy and is used in soups, salads, stir-fries and curries.

VEGETABLES

As well as the many vegetables such as carrots, broccoli and beansprouts that are commonly found in the West, there are some more unusual ones that are widely used in the Thai kitchen. They can be found in specialist Asian stores and some larger supermarkets.

Shallots

Thai shallots have a pinkish tinge and are smaller and more pungent than those seen in the West. They are used in a wide variety of dishes, while deep-fried shallots are used as a garnish.

Below: Thai shallots are an essential ingredient, and are used in spice pastes, soups, stir-fries and curries.

Salted eggs

These preserved duck eggs are served as an accompaniment. They are very salty, so one egg will serve several people. They are available from Asian stores and will keep for about 1 month.

Chinese leaves/Chinese cabbage

This mild, sweet vegetable has long, crinkled pale green leaves with a crunchy white central rib. It is widely available and is used in salads, soups and stir-fries. It can be stored in the refrigerator for several weeks.

Chinese broccoli

Similar to purple sprouting broccoli, this vegetable has long slender stems, loose leaves and a cluster of tiny white flowers at its centre. It has a peppery, cabbage-like flavour and may be served on its own as a side dish or added to soups, stir-fries and curries. Use quickly because it deteriorates.

Morning glory

Also known as water convolvulus or water spinach, this leafy vegetable has long, narrow green leaves with slender stems. It tastes rather like spinach. It does not keep well, so use as soon as possible after purchase.

Pak choi/Bok choy

This member of the cabbage family has broad white stems topped with lush dark green leaves. It has a slightly peppery flavour and may be eaten raw, or cooked in soups and stir-fries. Store in the refrigerator for 2–3 days.

Mushrooms

Many different types of mushroom are used in Thai salads, soups, stir-fries and curries. Button (white), chestnut, oyster and shiitake mushrooms are available fresh and can be stored in a paper bag in the refrigerator for a few days. Shiitake mushrooms are also available dried and should be soaked in boiling water before use. Tiny straw mushrooms are available in cans.

Aubergine/Eggplant

Several different types of aubergine are used in Thailand: long aubergines, small round apple aubergines and tiny pea aubergines. Depending on variety, they vary from white to pale green and purple. They are used in many different dishes, including curries and stir-fries.

Bamboo shoots

These creamy white shoots have a crisp texture and mild flavour and are used in salads, soups, stir-fries and curries. They are available canned and should be drained and rinsed well before use.

Mooli/Daikon

This long white root has a crisp, juicy texture and mild, peppery flavour rather like radish. It may be grated in salads or added to soups, stir-fries and curries. It should be peeled before use.

Snake beans/Yard long beans

Also known as asparagus beans or Thai beans, these resemble exceptionally long green beans – with many growing up to 40cm/16in. They may be pale or dark green; the latter are tastier. Try to choose young, narrow beans with underdeveloped seeds because older beans tend to be tough. Store in the refrigerator and use within 3 days of purchase, before they turn yellow.

Below: Morning glory is a very popular vegetable in Thailand. It is eaten raw, or cooked in soups and stir-fries.

Above: When buying rambutans, look out for brightly coloured fruits with green-tipped hairs.

FRUIT

As well as common tropical fruits such as mangoes and lychees, Thai cooks use many other, more unusual fruits that are available from Asian stores.

Asian pear

These round pears have a golden-brown skin and crisp, juicy white flesh. They are good eaten raw, but are also used in savoury salads. Store in the refrigerator.

Papaya

Also known as a paw-paw, this sweet, scented fruit has meltingly tender flesh surrounding a clutch of shiny black seeds. To prepare the ripe fruit, halve and scoop out the seeds. Choose unblemished ripe fruit that is orange all over or, if you do not plan to use it immediately, choose slightly firm fruit with a greenish skin that is turning orange. Ripe papayas will keep in the refrigerator for about a week. Unripe, or green, papaya is used as a vegetable in salads, soups and curries.

Pitaya/Dragon fruit

These stunning bright pink or yellow fruits have green-tipped scales. Inside, the flesh is white, specked with tiny black, edible seeds. It has a crisp texture and mild flavour. Ripe fruit should yield slightly when squeezed.

Pomelo

There are several varieties of this very large, round citrus fruit. The fruits may have a greenish-yellow rind and creamy white flesh, or dark green rind and sweet, juicy, pink flesh. The fruit may be eaten on its own or used in salads. Whole, unpeeled fruits will keep at room temperature for about 1 month.

Rambutan

This "hairy" red-skinned fruit has a translucent white flesh with a sweet, scented flavour like lychee surrounding a large stone (pit). They can be stored in the refrigerator for up to 1 week.

NUTS AND SEEDS

Many different nuts and seeds are used in Thai cooking. Peanuts are often crushed and added to sauces and spicy curries, while cashew nuts may be used whole. Sesame seeds add a wonderful rich flavour to many dishes including salads, stir-fries and curries.

Banana flower

Also called banana blossom or banana bud, this is actually the unopened heart of the banana flower. It has a mild taste and tender texture rather like an artichoke heart, and is used in salads and soups. Banana flowers are available fresh, canned or dried. Once cut, the fresh flower discolours, so brush with lemon juice to prevent it turning brown.

APPETIZERS AND SOUPS

Wander around the streets in any Thai city or town and you will see vendors standing behind portable cooking carts or squatting beside burners with battered woks ready to receive garlic, ginger, chillies and vegetables. The smells are enticing and those who are tempted to taste are seldom disappointed. The good news is that you don't have to travel to try these treats. Follow these simple recipes for delicious appetizers and soups such as Firecrackers and Hot-and-sour Prawn Soup.

CHICKEN SATAY <u>WITH</u> PEANUT SAUCE

THESE MINIATURE KEBABS ARE POPULAR ALL OVER SOUTH-EAST ASIA, AND THEY ARE ESPECIALLY DELICIOUS WHEN COOKED ON A BARBECUE. THE PEANUT DIPPING SAUCE IS A PERFECT PARTNER FOR THE MARINATED CHICKEN.

SERVES FOUR

INGREDIENTS
    4 skinless, boneless chicken
        breast portions
For the marinade
    2 garlic cloves, crushed
    2.5cm/1in piece fresh root ginger,
        finely grated
    10ml/2 tsp Thai fish sauce
    30ml/2 tbsp light soy sauce
    15ml/1 tbsp clear honey
For the satay sauce
    90ml/6 tbsp crunchy peanut butter
    1 fresh red chilli, seeded and
        finely chopped
    juice of 1 lime
    60ml/4 tbsp coconut milk
    salt

1 First, make the satay sauce. Put all the ingredients in a food processor or blender. Process until smooth, then check the seasoning and add more salt or lime juice if necessary. Spoon the sauce into a bowl, cover with clear film (plastic wrap) and set aside.

2 Using a sharp knife, slice each chicken breast portion into four long strips. Put all the marinade ingredients in a large bowl and mix well, then add the chicken strips and toss together until thoroughly coated. Cover and leave for at least 30 minutes in the refrigerator to marinate. Meanwhile, soak 16 wooden satay sticks or kebab skewers in water, to prevent them from burning during cooking.

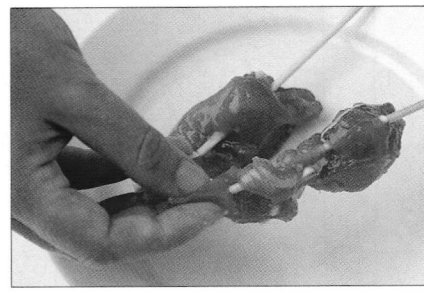

3 Preheat the grill (broiler) to high or prepare the barbecue. Drain the satay sticks or skewers. Drain the chicken strips. Thread one strip on to each satay stick or skewer. Grill (broil) for 3 minutes on each side, or until the chicken is golden brown and cooked through. Serve immediately with the satay sauce.

POTATO, SHALLOT <u>AND</u> GARLIC SAMOSAS <u>WITH</u> GREEN PEAS

MOST SAMOSAS ARE DEEP-FRIED. THESE ARE BAKED, MAKING THEM A HEALTHIER OPTION. THEY ARE ALSO PERFECT FOR PARTIES, SINCE THE PASTRIES NEED NO LAST-MINUTE ATTENTION.

MAKES TWENTY-FIVE

INGREDIENTS
1 large potato, about 250g/
   9oz, diced
15ml/1 tbsp groundnut
   (peanut) oil
2 shallots, finely chopped
1 garlic clove, finely chopped
60ml/4 tbsp coconut milk
5ml/1 tsp Thai red or green
   curry paste
75g/3oz/¾ cup peas
juice of ½ lime
25 samosa wrappers or 10 x 5cm/
   4 x 2in strips of filo pastry
salt and ground black pepper
oil, for brushing

1 Preheat the oven to 220°C/425°F/ Gas 7. Bring a small pan of water to the boil, add the diced potato, cover and cook for 10–15 minutes, until tender. Drain and set aside.

2 Meanwhile, heat the groundnut oil in a large frying pan and cook the shallots and garlic over a medium heat, stirring occasionally, for 4–5 minutes, until softened and golden.

3 Add the drained diced potato, coconut milk, red or green curry paste, peas and lime juice to the frying pan. Mash together coarsely with a wooden spoon. Season to taste with salt and pepper and cook over a low heat for 2–3 minutes, then remove the pan from the heat and set aside until the mixture has cooled a little.

4 Lay a samosa wrapper or filo strip flat on the work surface. Brush with a little oil, then place a generous teaspoonful of the mixture in the middle of one end. Turn one corner diagonally over the filling to meet the long edge.

5 Continue folding over the filling, keeping the triangular shape as you work down the strip. Brush with a little more oil if necessary and place on a baking sheet. Prepare all the other samosas in the same way.

6 Bake for 15 minutes, or until the pastry is golden and crisp. Leave to cool slightly before serving.

COOK'S TIP
Many Asian food stores sell what is described as a samosa pad. This is a packet, usually frozen, containing about 50 oblong pieces of samosa pastry. Filo pastry, cut to size, can be used instead.

FIRECRACKERS

IT'S EASY TO SEE HOW THESE PASTRY-WRAPPED PRAWN SNACKS GOT THEIR NAME (KRATHAK IN THAI)
— AS WELL AS RESEMBLING FIREWORKS, THEIR CONTENTS EXPLODE WITH FLAVOUR.

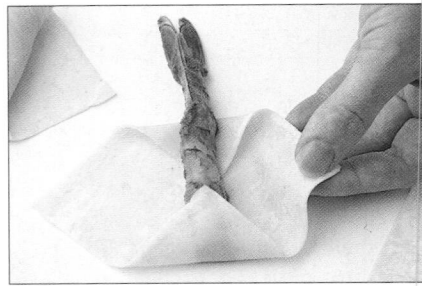

3 Place a wonton wrapper on the work surface at an angle so that it forms a diamond shape, then fold the top corner over so that the point is in the centre. Place a prawn, slits down, on the wrapper, with the tail projecting from the folded end, then fold the bottom corner over the other end of the prawn.

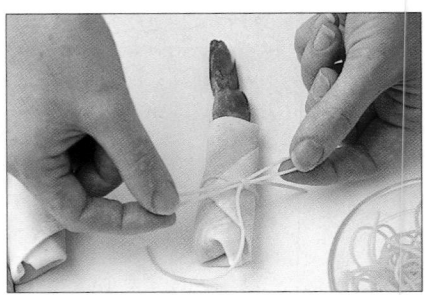

4 Fold each side of the wrapper over in turn to make a tightly folded roll. Tie a noodle in a bow around the roll and set it aside. Repeat with the remaining prawns and wrappers.

5 Heat the oil in a deep-fryer or wok to 190°C/375°F or until a cube of bread, added to the oil, browns in 45 seconds. Fry the prawns, a few at a time, for 5–8 minutes, until golden brown and cooked through. Drain well on kitchen paper and keep hot while you cook the remaining batches.

COOK'S TIP
Soak the fine egg noodles used as ties for the prawn rolls in a bowl of boiling water for 2–3 minutes, until softened, then drain, refresh under cold running water and drain well again.

MAKES SIXTEEN

INGREDIENTS
  16 large, raw king prawns (jumbo shrimp), heads and shells removed but tails left on
  5ml/1 tsp red curry paste
  15ml/1 tbsp Thai fish sauce
  16 small wonton wrappers, about 8cm/3¼in square, thawed if frozen
  16 fine egg noodles, soaked (see Cook's Tip)
  oil, for deep-frying

1 Place the prawns on their sides and cut two slits through the underbelly of each, one about 1cm/½in from the head end and the other about 1cm/½in from the first cut, cutting across the prawn. This will prevent the prawns from curling when they are cooked.

2 Mix the curry paste with the fish sauce in a shallow dish. Add the prawns and turn them in the mixture until they are well coated. Cover and leave to marinate for 10 minutes.

GREEN CURRY PUFFS

SHRIMP PASTE AND GREEN CURRY SAUCE, USED JUDICIOUSLY, GIVE THESE PUFFS THEIR DISTINCTIVE, SPICY, SAVOURY FLAVOUR, AND THE ADDITION OF CHILLI STEPS UP THE HEAT.

MAKES TWENTY-FOUR

INGREDIENTS
- 24 small wonton wrappers, about 8cm/3¼ in square, thawed if frozen
- 15ml/1 tbsp cornflour (cornstarch), mixed to a paste with 30ml/ 2 tbsp water
- oil, for deep-frying

For the filling
- 1 small potato, about 115g/4oz, boiled and mashed
- 25g/1oz/3 tbsp cooked petits pois (baby peas)
- 25g/1oz/3 tbsp cooked corn
- few sprigs fresh coriander (cilantro), chopped
- 1 small fresh red chilli, seeded and finely chopped
- ½ lemon grass stalk, finely chopped
- 15ml/1 tbsp soy sauce
- 5ml/1 tsp shrimp paste or fish sauce
- 5ml/1 tsp Thai green curry paste

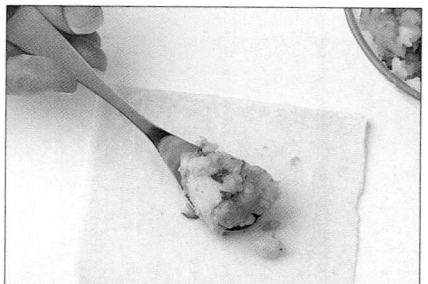

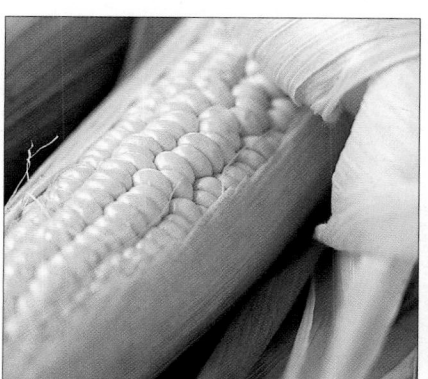

1 Combine the filling ingredients. Lay out one wonton wrapper and place a teaspoon of the filling in the centre.

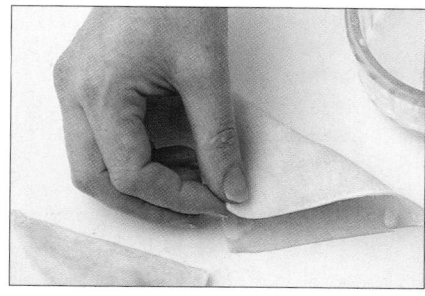

2 Brush a little of the cornflour paste along two sides of the square. Fold the other two sides over to meet them, then press together to make a triangular pastry and seal in the filling. Make more pastries in the same way.

3 Heat the oil in a deep-fryer or wok to 190°C/375°F or until a cube of bread, added to the oil, browns in about 45 seconds. Add the pastries to the oil, a few at a time, and fry them for about 5 minutes, until golden brown.

4 Remove from the fryer or wok and drain on kitchen paper. If you intend serving the puffs hot, place them in a low oven while cooking successive batches. The puffs also taste good cold.

COOK'S TIP
Wonton wrappers dry out quickly, so keep them covered, using clear film (plastic wrap), until you are ready to use them.

FISH CAKES <u>WITH</u> CUCUMBER RELISH

THESE WONDERFUL SMALL FISH CAKES ARE A VERY FAMILIAR AND POPULAR APPETIZER IN THAILAND AND INCREASINGLY THROUGHOUT SOUTH-EAST ASIA. THEY ARE USUALLY SERVED WITH THAI BEER.

MAKES ABOUT TWELVE

INGREDIENTS
8 kaffir lime leaves
300g/11oz cod fillet, cut into chunks
30ml/2 tbsp red curry paste
1 egg
30ml/2 tbsp Thai fish sauce
5ml/1 tsp granulated sugar
30ml/2 tbsp cornflour (cornstarch)
15ml/1 tbsp chopped fresh
   coriander (cilantro)
50g/2oz/½ cup green beans,
   thinly sliced
vegetable oil, for deep-frying
For the cucumber relish
60ml/4 tbsp coconut or rice vinegar
50g/2oz/¼ cup granulated sugar
60ml/4 tbsp water
1 head pickled garlic
1cm/½ in piece fresh root
   ginger, peeled
1 cucumber, cut into thin batons
4 shallots, thinly sliced

1 Make the cucumber relish. Mix the coconut or rice vinegar, sugar and water in a small pan. Heat gently, stirring constantly until the sugar has completely dissolved. Remove the pan from the heat and leave to cool.

2 Separate the pickled garlic into cloves. Chop the cloves finely, along with the ginger, and place in a bowl. Add the cucumber batons and shallots, pour over the vinegar mixture and mix lightly. Cover and set aside.

3 Reserve five kaffir lime leaves for the garnish and thinly slice the remainder. Put the chunks of fish, curry paste and egg in a food processor and process to a smooth paste. Transfer the mixture to a bowl and stir in the fish sauce, sugar, cornflour, sliced kaffir lime leaves, coriander and green beans. Mix well, then shape the mixture into about twelve 5mm/¼in thick cakes, each measuring about 5cm/2in in diameter.

4 Heat the oil in a deep-frying pan or wok to 190°C/375°F or until a cube of bread, added to the oil, browns in about 45 seconds. Fry the fish cakes, a few at a time, for about 4–5 minutes, until cooked and evenly brown.

5 Lift out the fish cakes and drain them on kitchen paper. Keep each batch hot while frying successive batches. Garnish with the reserved kaffir lime leaves and serve with the cucumber relish.

THAI SPRING ROLLS

CRUNCHY SPRING ROLLS ARE AS POPULAR IN THAILAND AS THEY ARE IN CHINA. THAIS FILL THEIR VERSION WITH A DELICIOUS GARLIC, PORK AND NOODLE MIXTURE.

MAKES TWENTY-FOUR

INGREDIENTS
  24 x 15cm/6in square spring roll
    wrappers, thawed if frozen
  30ml/2 tbsp plain (all-purpose) flour
  vegetable oil, for deep-frying
  sweet chilli dipping sauce,
    to serve
For the filling
  4–6 Chinese dried mushrooms,
    soaked for 30 minutes in warm
    water to cover
  50g/2oz cellophane noodles
  30ml/2 tbsp vegetable oil
  2 garlic cloves, chopped
  2 fresh red chillies, seeded
    and chopped
  225g/8oz minced (ground) pork
  50g/2oz peeled cooked prawns
    (shrimp), thawed if frozen
  30ml/2 tbsp Thai fish sauce
  5ml/1 tsp granulated sugar
  1 carrot, grated
  50g/2oz piece of canned bamboo
    shoot, drained and chopped
  50g/2oz/⅔ cup beansprouts
  2 spring onions (scallions),
    finely chopped
  15ml/1 tbsp chopped fresh
    coriander (cilantro)
  ground black pepper

1 Make the filling. Drain the soaked mushrooms. Cut off and discard the stems, then chop the caps finely.

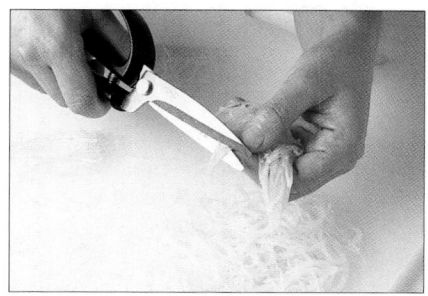

2 Place the noodles in a large bowl, cover with boiling water and soak for 10 minutes. Drain the noodles and snip them into 5cm/2in lengths.

3 Heat the oil in a wok, add the garlic and chillies and stir-fry for 30 seconds. Transfer to a plate. Add the pork to the wok and stir-fry until it has browned.

4 Add the mushrooms, noodles and prawns. Stir in the fish sauce and sugar, then add pepper to taste.

5 Transfer the mixture to a bowl. Stir in the grated carrot, chopped bamboo shoot, beansprouts, spring onions and chopped coriander. Add the reserved chilli mixture and mix well.

6 Unwrap the spring roll wrappers. Cover them with a dampened dishtowel while you are making the rolls, so that they do not dry out, and work on them one at a time. Put the flour in a small bowl and stir in a little water to make a paste. Place a spoonful of the filling in the centre of a spring roll wrapper.

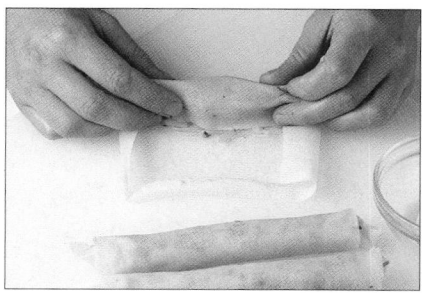

7 Turn the bottom edge over to cover the filling, then fold in the sides. Roll up the wrapper almost to the top, then brush the top edge with the flour paste and seal. Fill the remaining wrappers.

8 Heat the oil in a deep-fryer or wok to 190°C/375°F or until a cube of bread browns in about 45 seconds. Fry the spring rolls, in batches, until crisp and golden. Drain on kitchen paper and serve hot with sweet chilli sauce.

GALANGAL, CHICKEN AND COCONUT SOUP

THIS AROMATIC SOUP IS RICH WITH COCONUT MILK AND INTENSELY FLAVOURED WITH GALANGAL, LEMON GRASS AND KAFFIR LIME LEAVES.

SERVES FOUR TO SIX

INGREDIENTS

    4 lemon grass stalks, roots trimmed
    2 x 400ml/14fl oz cans coconut milk
    475ml/16fl oz/2 cups chicken stock
    2.5cm/1in piece fresh galangal,
      peeled and thinly sliced
    10 black peppercorns, crushed
    10 kaffir lime leaves, torn
    300g/11oz skinless, boneless chicken
      breast portions, cut into thin strips
    115g/4oz/1 cup button (white)
      mushrooms, halved if large
    50g/2oz/½ cup baby corn cobs,
      quartered lengthways
    60ml/4 tbsp fresh lime juice
    45ml/3 tbsp Thai fish sauce
    chopped fresh red chillies, spring
      onions (scallions) and fresh
      coriander (cilantro) leaves,
      to garnish

1 Cut off the lower 5cm/2in from each lemon grass stalk and chop it finely. Bruise the remaining pieces of stalk. Bring the coconut milk and chicken stock to the boil in a large pan over a medium heat. Add the chopped and bruised lemon grass, the galangal, peppercorns and half the kaffir lime leaves, reduce the heat to low and simmer gently for 10 minutes. Strain the soup into a clean pan.

2 Return the soup to a low heat, then stir in the chicken strips, mushrooms and corn. Simmer gently, stirring occasionally, for 5–7 minutes, or until the chicken is cooked.

3 Stir in the lime juice and fish sauce, then add the remaining lime leaves. Ladle into warm bowls and serve, garnished with chopped chillies, spring onions and coriander leaves.

HOT-AND-SOUR PRAWN SOUP

THIS IS A CLASSIC THAI SEAFOOD SOUP – TOM YAM KUNG – AND IT IS ONE OF THE MOST POPULAR AND BEST-KNOWN THAI SOUPS.

SERVES FOUR TO SIX

INGREDIENTS

    450g/1lb raw king prawns (jumbo
      shrimp), thawed if frozen
    1 litre/1¾ pints/4 cups chicken
      stock or water
    3 lemon grass stalks,
      roots trimmed
    10 kaffir lime leaves,
      torn in half
    225g/8oz can straw
      mushrooms, drained
    45ml/3 tbsp Thai fish sauce
    60ml/4 tbsp fresh lime juice
    30ml/2 tbsp chopped spring
      onion (scallion)
    15ml/1 tbsp fresh coriander
      (cilantro) leaves
    4 fresh red chillies, seeded
      and thinly sliced
    salt and ground black pepper

1 Peel the prawns, reserving the shells. Devein the prawns and set aside.

2 Rinse the shells under cold water, then put them in a large pan with the stock or water. Bring to the boil.

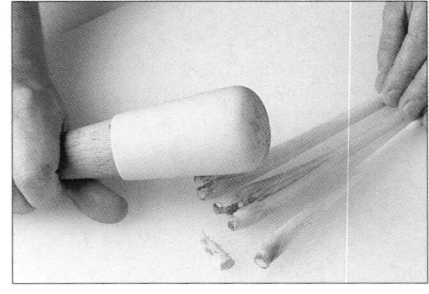

3 Bruise the lemon grass stalks and add them to the stock with half the lime leaves. Simmer gently for 5–6 minutes, until the stock is fragrant.

4 Strain the stock, return it to the clean pan and reheat. Add the drained mushrooms and the prawns, then cook until the prawns turn pink.

5 Stir the fish sauce, lime juice, spring onion, coriander, chillies and the remaining lime leaves into the soup. Taste and adjust the seasoning if necessary. The soup should be sour, salty, spicy and hot.

CELLOPHANE NOODLE SOUP

THE NOODLES USED IN THIS SOUP GO BY VARIOUS NAMES: GLASS NOODLES, CELLOPHANE NOODLES, BEAN THREAD OR TRANSPARENT NOODLES. THEY ARE ESPECIALLY VALUED FOR THEIR BRITTLE TEXTURE.

SERVES FOUR

INGREDIENTS
    4 large dried shiitake mushrooms
    15g/½oz dried lily buds
    ½ cucumber, coarsely chopped
    2 garlic cloves, halved
    90g/3½oz white cabbage, chopped
    1.2 litres/2 pints/5 cups
        boiling water
    115g/4oz cellophane noodles
    30ml/2 tbsp soy sauce
    15ml/1 tbsp palm sugar or light
        muscovado (brown) sugar
    90g/3½oz block silken tofu, diced
    fresh coriander (cilantro) leaves,
        to garnish

1 Soak the shiitake mushrooms in warm water for 30 minutes. In a separate bowl, soak the dried lily buds in warm water, also for 30 minutes.

2 Meanwhile, put the cucumber, garlic and cabbage in a food processor and process to a smooth paste. Scrape the mixture into a large pan and add the measured boiling water.

3 Bring to the boil, then reduce the heat and cook for 2 minutes, stirring occasionally. Strain this stock into another pan, return to a low heat and bring to simmering point.

4 Drain the lily buds, rinse under cold running water, then drain again. Cut off any hard ends. Add the lily buds to the stock with the noodles, soy sauce and sugar and cook for 5 minutes more.

5 Strain the mushroom soaking liquid into the soup. Discard the mushroom stems, then slice the caps. Divide them and the tofu among four bowls. Pour the soup over, garnish and serve.

CHIANG MAI NOODLE SOUP

NOWADAYS A SIGNATURE DISH OF THE CITY OF CHIANG MAI, THIS DELICIOUS NOODLE SOUP ORIGINATED IN BURMA, NOW CALLED MYANMAR, WHICH LIES ONLY A LITTLE TO THE NORTH.

SERVES FOUR TO SIX

INGREDIENTS
  600ml/1 pint/2½ cups coconut milk
  30ml/2 tbsp Thai red curry paste
  5ml/1 tsp ground turmeric
  450g/1lb chicken thighs, boned and
    cut into bitesize chunks
  600ml/1 pint/2½ cups
    chicken stock
  60ml/4 tbsp Thai fish sauce
  15ml/1 tbsp dark soy sauce
  juice of ½–1 lime
  450g/1lb fresh egg noodles,
    blanched briefly in boiling water
  salt and ground black pepper
To garnish
  3 spring onions (scallions),
    chopped
  4 fresh red chillies, chopped
  4 shallots, chopped
  60ml/4 tbsp sliced pickled mustard
    leaves, rinsed
  30ml/2 tbsp fried sliced garlic
  coriander (cilantro) leaves
  4–6 fried noodle nests (optional)

1 Pour about one-third of the coconut milk into a large, heavy pan or wok. Bring to the boil over a medium heat, stirring frequently with a wooden spoon until the milk separates.

2 Add the curry paste and ground turmeric, stir to mix completely and cook until the mixture is fragrant.

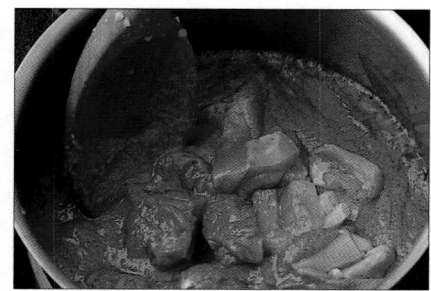

3 Add the chunks of chicken and toss over the heat for about 2 minutes, making sure that all the chunks are thoroughly coated with the paste.

4 Add the remaining coconut milk, the chicken stock, fish sauce and soy sauce. Season with salt and pepper to taste. Bring to simmering point, stirring frequently, then lower the heat and cook gently for 7–10 minutes. Remove from the heat and stir in lime juice to taste.

5 Reheat the fresh egg noodles in boiling water, drain and divide among four to six warmed bowls. Divide the chunks of chicken among the bowls and ladle in the hot soup. Top each serving with spring onions, chillies, shallots, pickled mustard leaves, fried garlic, coriander leaves and a fried noodle nest, if using. Serve immediately.

SALADS

Like all hot countries, Thailand has a fine repertoire of salads
and cold dishes. These aren't salads in the Western sense, but
rather combinations of fresh and cooked vegetables, often with
a little chicken, beef or seafood. Dressings are seldom oil-based.
Instead, they tend to be tart and spicy mixtures, made by
adding Thai fish sauce to lime juice, tamarind juice or a little
rice vinegar. Salads can be served as a side dish or appetizer,
or as a main course with noodles or rice.

AUBERGINE SALAD WITH SHRIMP AND EGG

An appetizing and unusual salad that you will find yourself making over and over again. Roasting the aubergines really brings out their flavour.

SERVES FOUR TO SIX

INGREDIENTS
2 aubergines (eggplants)
15ml/1 tbsp vegetable oil
30ml/2 tbsp dried shrimp, soaked in warm water for 10 minutes
15ml/1 tbsp coarsely chopped garlic
1 hard-boiled egg, chopped
4 shallots, thinly sliced into rings
fresh coriander (cilantro) leaves and 2 fresh red chillies, seeded and sliced, to garnish
For the dressing
30ml/2 tbsp fresh lime juice
5ml/1 tsp palm sugar or light muscovado (brown) sugar
30ml/2 tbsp Thai fish sauce

1 Preheat the grill (broiler) to medium or preheat the oven to 180°C/350°F/ Gas 4. Prick the aubergines several times with a skewer, then arrange on a baking sheet. Cook them under the grill for 30–40 minutes, or until they are charred and tender. Alternatively, roast them by placing them directly on the shelf of the oven for about 1 hour, turning them at least twice. Remove the aubergines and set aside until they are cool enough to handle.

2 Meanwhile, make the dressing. Put the lime juice, palm or muscovado sugar and fish sauce into a small bowl. Whisk well with a fork or balloon whisk. Cover with clear film (plastic wrap) and set aside until required.

3 When the aubergines are cool enough to handle, peel off the skin and cut the flesh into medium slices.

4 Heat the oil in a small frying pan. Drain the dried shrimp thoroughly and add them to the pan with the garlic. Cook over a medium heat for about 3 minutes, until golden. Remove from the pan and set aside.

5 Arrange the aubergine slices on a serving dish. Top with the hard-boiled egg, shallots and dried shrimp mixture. Drizzle over the dressing and garnish with the coriander and red chillies.

VARIATION
For a special occasion, use salted duck's or quail's eggs, cut in half, instead of chopped hen's eggs.

SEAFOOD SALAD WITH FRAGRANT HERBS

THIS IS A SPECTACULAR SALAD. THE LUSCIOUS COMBINATION OF PRAWNS, SCALLOPS AND SQUID MAKES IT THE IDEAL CHOICE FOR A SPECIAL CELEBRATION.

SERVES FOUR TO SIX

INGREDIENTS

250ml/8fl oz/1 cup fish stock
  or water
350g/12oz squid, cleaned and cut
  into rings
12 raw king prawns (jumbo shrimp),
  peeled, with tails intact
12 scallops
50g/2oz cellophane noodles, soaked
  in warm water for 30 minutes
½ cucumber, cut into thin batons
1 lemon grass stalk, finely chopped
2 kaffir lime leaves, finely shredded
2 shallots, thinly sliced
30ml/2 tbsp chopped spring
  onions (scallions)
30ml/2 tbsp fresh coriander
  (cilantro) leaves
12–15 fresh mint leaves,
  coarsely torn
4 fresh red chillies, seeded and cut
  into slivers
juice of 1–2 limes
30ml/2 tbsp Thai fish sauce
fresh coriander sprigs, to garnish

1 Pour the fish stock or water into a medium pan, set over a high heat and bring to the boil. Cook each type of seafood separately in the stock for 3–4 minutes. Remove with a slotted spoon and set aside to cool.

2 Drain the noodles. Using scissors, cut them into short lengths, about 5cm/2in long. Place them in a serving bowl and add the cucumber, lemon grass, kaffir lime leaves, shallots, spring onions, coriander, mint and chillies.

3 Pour over the lime juice and fish sauce. Mix well, then add the seafood. Toss lightly. Garnish with the fresh coriander sprigs and serve.

PIQUANT PRAWN SALAD

THE FISH SAUCE DRESSING ADDS A SUPERB FLAVOUR TO THE NOODLES AND PRAWNS. THIS DELICIOUS SALAD CAN BE ENJOYED WARM OR COLD, AND WILL SERVE SIX AS AN APPETIZER.

SERVES FOUR

INGREDIENTS
200g/7oz rice vermicelli
8 baby corn cobs, halved
150g/5oz mangetouts (snow peas)
15ml/1 tbsp vegetable oil
2 garlic cloves, finely chopped
2.5cm/1in piece fresh root ginger,
  peeled and finely chopped
1 fresh red or green chilli, seeded
  and finely chopped
450g/1lb raw peeled tiger prawns
  (jumbo shrimp)
4 spring onions (scallions), very
  thinly sliced
15ml/1 tbsp sesame seeds, toasted
1 lemon grass stalk, thinly shredded
For the dressing
15ml/1 tbsp chopped fresh chives
15ml/1 tbsp Thai fish sauce
5ml/1 tsp soy sauce
45ml/3 tbsp groundnut (peanut) oil
5ml/1 tsp sesame oil
30ml/2 tbsp rice vinegar

1 Put the rice vermicelli in a wide heatproof bowl, pour over boiling water and leave to soak for 10 minutes. Drain, refresh under cold water and drain well again. Place in a large serving bowl and set aside until required.

2 Boil or steam the corn cobs and mangetouts for about 3 minutes, until tender but still crunchy. Refresh under cold running water and drain. Make the dressing by mixing all the ingredients in a screw-top jar. Close tightly and shake vigorously to combine.

3 Heat the oil in a large frying pan or wok. Add the garlic, ginger and red or green chilli and cook for 1 minute. Add the tiger prawns and toss over the heat for about 3 minutes, until they have just turned pink. Stir in the spring onions, corn cobs, mangetouts and sesame seeds, and toss lightly to mix.

4 Tip the contents of the pan or wok over the rice vermicelli. Pour the dressing on top and toss well. Sprinkle with lemon grass and serve, or chill for 1 hour before serving.

TANGY CHICKEN SALAD

THIS FRESH AND LIVELY DISH TYPIFIES THE CHARACTER OF THAI CUISINE. IT IS IDEAL FOR A LIGHT LUNCH ON A HOT AND LAZY SUMMER'S DAY.

SERVES FOUR TO SIX

INGREDIENTS

    4 skinless, boneless chicken
      breast portions
    2 garlic cloves, crushed
    30ml/2 tbsp soy sauce
    30ml/2 tbsp vegetable oil
    120ml/4fl oz/½ cup coconut
      cream
    30ml/2 tbsp Thai fish sauce
    juice of 1 lime
    30ml/2 tbsp palm sugar or light
      muscovado (brown) sugar
    115g/4oz/½ cup water
      chestnuts, sliced
    50g/2oz/½ cup cashew nuts, roasted
      and coarsely chopped
    4 shallots, thinly sliced
    4 kaffir lime leaves, thinly sliced
    1 lemon grass stalk, thinly sliced
    5ml/1 tsp chopped fresh galangal
    1 large fresh red chilli, seeded and
      finely chopped
    2 spring onions (scallions),
      thinly sliced
    10–12 fresh mint leaves, torn
    1 lettuce, separated into leaves,
      to serve
    2 fresh red chillies, seeded and
      sliced, to garnish

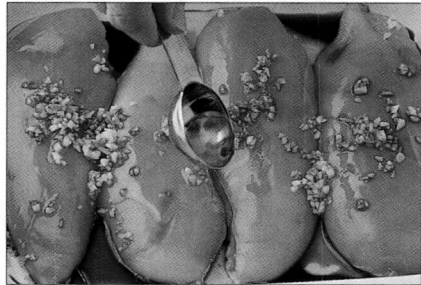

1 Place the chicken in a large dish. Rub with the garlic, soy sauce and 15ml/ 1 tbsp of the oil. Cover and leave to marinate for 1–2 hours.

2 Heat the remaining oil in a wok or frying pan and stir-fry the chicken for 3–4 minutes on each side, or until cooked. Remove and set aside to cool.

3 In a pan, heat the coconut cream, fish sauce, lime juice and sugar. Stir until the sugar has dissolved; set aside.

4 Tear the cooked chicken into strips and put it in a bowl. Add the water chestnuts, cashew nuts, shallots, kaffir lime leaves, lemon grass, galangal, red chilli, spring onions and mint leaves.

5 Pour the coconut dressing over the mixture and toss well. Serve the chicken on a bed of lettuce leaves and garnish with sliced red chillies.

LARP OF CHIANG MAI

CHIANG MAI IS A CITY IN THE NORTH-EAST OF THAILAND. THE CITY IS CULTURALLY VERY CLOSE TO LAOS. IT IS FAMOUS FOR ITS CHICKEN SALAD, WHICH WAS ORIGINALLY CALLED "LAAP" OR "LARP". DUCK, BEEF OR PORK CAN BE USED INSTEAD OF CHICKEN.

SERVES FOUR TO SIX

INGREDIENTS

    450g/1lb minced (ground) chicken
    1 lemon grass stalk, root trimmed
    3 kaffir lime leaves, finely chopped
    4 fresh red chillies, seeded
      and chopped
    60ml/4 tbsp fresh lime juice
    30ml/2 tbsp Thai fish sauce
    15ml/1 tbsp roasted ground rice (see
      Cook's Tip)
    2 spring onions (scallions),
      finely chopped
    30ml/2 tbsp fresh coriander
      (cilantro) leaves
    thinly sliced kaffir lime leaves, mixed
      salad leaves and fresh mint sprigs,
      to garnish

1 Heat a large, non-stick frying pan. Add the minced chicken and moisten with a little water. Stir constantly over a medium heat for 7–10 minutes, until it is cooked through. Remove the pan from the heat and drain off any excess fat. Cut off the lower 5cm/2in of the lemon grass stalk and chop it finely.

2 Transfer the cooked chicken to a bowl and add the chopped lemon grass, lime leaves, chillies, lime juice, fish sauce, roasted ground rice, spring onions and coriander. Mix thoroughly.

3 Spoon the chicken mixture into a salad bowl. Sprinkle sliced lime leaves over the top and garnish with salad leaves and sprigs of mint.

COOK'S TIP
Use glutinous rice for the roasted ground rice. Put the rice in a frying pan and dry-roast it until golden brown. Remove and grind to a powder, using a mortar and pestle or a food processor. When the rice is cold, store it in a glass jar in a cool and dry place.

THAI BEEF SALAD

A HEARTY MAIN MEAL SALAD, THIS COMBINES TENDER STRIPS OF SIRLOIN STEAK WITH THINLY SHREDDED CUCUMBER AND A WONDERFULLY PIQUANT CHILLI AND LIME DRESSING.

SERVES FOUR

INGREDIENTS

    2 sirloin steaks, each
      about 225g/8oz
    1 lemon grass stalk, root trimmed
    1 red onion or 4 Thai shallots,
      thinly sliced
    ½ cucumber, cut into strips
    30ml/2 tbsp chopped spring
      onion (scallion)
    juice of 2 limes
    15–30ml/1–2 tbsp Thai fish sauce
    2–4 fresh red chillies, seeded and
      finely chopped
    Chinese mustard cress, salad cress or
      fresh coriander (cilantro), to garnish

COOK'S TIP
Look for gui chai leaves in Thai and Chinese groceries. These look like very thin spring onions (scallions) and are often used as a substitute for the more familiar vegetable.

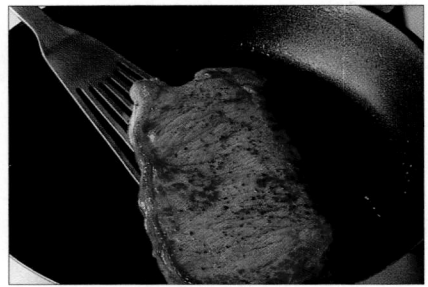

1 Pan-fry the steaks in a large, heavy frying pan over a medium heat. Cook them for 4–6 minutes for rare, 6–8 minutes for medium-rare and about 10 minutes for well done, depending on their thickness. (In Thailand the beef is traditionally served quite rare.) Alternatively, cook them under a preheated grill (broiler). Remove the steaks from the pan and leave to rest for 10–15 minutes. Meanwhile, cut off the lower 5cm/2in from the lemon grass stalk and chop it finely.

2 When the meat is cool, slice it thinly and put the slices in a large bowl. Add the sliced onion or shallots, cucumber, lemon grass and chopped spring onion to the meat slices.

3 Toss the salad and add lime juice and fish sauce to taste. Add the red chillies and toss again. Transfer to a serving bowl or plate. Serve the salad at room temperature or chilled, garnished with the Chinese mustard cress, salad cress or coriander leaves.

SAENG WA OF GRILLED PORK

*PORK FILLET IS CUT IN STRIPS BEFORE BEING GRILLED. SHREDDED AND THEN TOSSED WITH A
DELICIOUS SWEET-SOUR SAUCE, IT MAKES A MARVELLOUS WARM SALAD.*

3 Transfer the cooked pork strips to a board. Slice the meat across the grain, then shred it with a fork. Place in a large bowl and add the shallot slices, lemon grass, kaffir lime leaves, ginger, chilli and chopped coriander.

4 Make the dressing. Place the sugar, fish sauce, lime juice and tamarind juice in a bowl. Whisk until the sugar has completely dissolved. Pour the dressing over the pork mixture and toss well to mix, then serve.

VARIATION

If you want to extend this dish a little, add cooked rice or noodles. Thin strips of red or yellow (bell) pepper could also be added. For a colour contrast, add lightly cooked green beans, sugar snap peas or mangetouts (snow peas).

SERVES FOUR

INGREDIENTS
    30ml/2 tbsp dark soy sauce
    15ml/1 tbsp clear honey
    400g/14oz pork fillet (tenderloin)
    6 shallots, very thinly
      sliced lengthways
    1 lemon grass stalk, thinly sliced
    5 kaffir lime leaves, thinly sliced
    5cm/2in piece fresh root ginger,
      peeled and sliced into
      fine shreds
    ½ fresh long red chilli, seeded and
      sliced into fine shreds
    small bunch fresh coriander
      (cilantro), chopped
For the dressing
    30ml/2 tbsp palm sugar or light
      muscovado (brown) sugar
    30ml/2 tbsp Thai fish sauce
    juice of 2 limes
    20ml/4 tsp thick tamarind juice,
      made by mixing tamarind paste
      with warm water

1 Preheat the grill (broiler) to medium. Mix the soy sauce with the honey in a small bowl or jug (pitcher) and stir until the honey has completely dissolved.

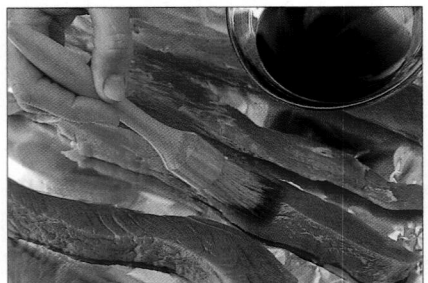

2 Using a sharp knife, cut the pork fillet lengthways into quarters to make four long, thick strips. Place the pork strips in a grill pan. Brush generously with the soy sauce and honey mixture, then grill (broil) for about 10–15 minutes, until cooked through and tender. Turn the strips over frequently and baste with the soy sauce and honey mixture.

BEEF AND MUSHROOM SALAD

ALL THE INGREDIENTS FOR THIS TRADITIONAL THAI DISH — KNOWN AS YAM NUA YANG *— ARE WIDELY AVAILABLE IN LARGER SUPERMARKETS.*

SERVES FOUR

INGREDIENTS

  675g/1½lb fillet (tenderloin) or
    rump (round) steak
  30ml/2 tbsp olive oil
  2 small mild red chillies, seeded
    and sliced
  225g/8oz/3¼ cups fresh shiitake
    mushrooms, stems removed and
    caps sliced
For the dressing
  3 spring onions (scallions),
    finely chopped
  2 garlic cloves, finely chopped
  juice of 1 lime
  15–30ml/1–2 tbsp Thai fish sauce
  5ml/1 tsp soft light brown sugar
  30ml/2 tbsp chopped fresh
    coriander (cilantro)
To serve
  1 cos or romaine lettuce, torn
    into strips
  175g/6oz cherry tomatoes, halved
  5cm/2in piece cucumber, peeled,
    halved and thinly sliced
  45ml/3 tbsp toasted sesame seeds

VARIATION
If you can find them, yellow chillies
make a colourful addition to this dish.

1 Preheat the grill (broiler) to medium,
then cook the steak for 2–4 minutes on
each side, depending on how well done
you like it. (In Thailand, the beef is
traditionally served quite rare.) Leave to
cool for at least 15 minutes.

2 Slice the meat as thinly as possible
and place the slices in a bowl.

3 Heat the olive oil in a small frying
pan. Add the seeded and sliced red
chillies and the sliced shiitake
mushroom caps. Cook for 5 minutes,
stirring occasionally. Turn off the heat
and add the steak slices to the pan.
Stir well to coat the beef slices in the
chilli and mushroom mixture.

4 Make the dressing by mixing all the
ingredients in a bowl, then pour it over
the meat mixture and toss gently.

5 Arrange the lettuce, tomatoes and
cucumber on a serving plate. Spoon the
steak mixture in the centre and sprinkle
the sesame seeds over. Serve at once.

VEGETABLE
MAIN DISHES

Thailand has never really had a vegetarian tradition, but there are many excellent vegetable dishes, often using nuts or tofu, which are very popular with Western vegetarians. Some of the recipes in this chapter use fish sauce, which should be omitted for vegetarians. Delicious vegetable curries, unusual stir-fries, stuffed vegetables and a fragrant stew are included here. Most are very quick and easy to make, with the majority of time required for preparation, rather than cooking.

TOFU AND VEGETABLE THAI CURRY

TRADITIONAL THAI INGREDIENTS — CHILLIES, GALANGAL, LEMON GRASS AND KAFFIR LIME LEAVES — GIVE THIS CURRY A WONDERFULLY FRAGRANT AROMA. THE TOFU NEEDS TO MARINATE FOR AT LEAST 2 HOURS, SO BEAR THIS IN MIND WHEN TIMING YOUR MEAL.

SERVES FOUR

INGREDIENTS
  175g/6oz firm tofu
  45ml/3 tbsp dark soy sauce
  15ml/1 tbsp sesame oil
  5ml/1 tsp chilli sauce
  2.5cm/1in piece fresh root ginger,
    peeled and finely grated
  1 head broccoli, about 225g/8oz
  ½ head cauliflower, about 225g/8oz
  30ml/2 tbsp vegetable oil
  1 onion, sliced
  400ml/14fl oz/1⅔ cups coconut milk
  150ml/¼ pint/⅔ cup water
  1 red (bell) pepper, seeded
    and chopped
  175g/6oz/generous 1 cup green
    beans, halved
  115g/4oz/1½ cups shiitake or button
    (white) mushrooms, halved
  shredded spring onions (scallions),
    to garnish
  boiled jasmine rice or noodles,
    to serve
For the curry paste
  2 fresh red or green chillies, seeded
    and chopped
  1 lemon grass stalk, chopped
  2.5cm/1in piece fresh
    galangal, chopped
  2 kaffir lime leaves
  10ml/2 tsp ground coriander
  a few fresh coriander (cilantro)
    sprigs, including the stalks
  45ml/3 tbsp water

1 Rinse and drain the tofu. Using a sharp knife, cut it into 2.5cm/1in cubes. Place the cubes in an ovenproof dish that is large enough to hold them all in a single layer.

2 Mix together the soy sauce, sesame oil, chilli sauce and grated ginger in a jug (pitcher) and pour over the tofu. Toss gently to coat all the cubes evenly, cover with clear film (plastic wrap) and leave to marinate for at least 2 hours or overnight if possible, turning and basting the tofu occasionally.

3 Make the curry paste. Place the chillies, lemon grass, galangal, lime leaves, ground coriander and fresh coriander in a food processor and process until well blended. Add the water and process to a thick paste.

4 Preheat the oven to 190°C/375°F/Gas 5. Cut the broccoli and cauliflower into small florets. Cut any stalks into thin slices.

5 Heat the vegetable oil in a frying pan and add the sliced onion. Cook over a low heat for about 8 minutes, until soft and lightly browned. Stir in the curry paste and the coconut milk. Add the water and bring to the boil.

6 Stir in the red pepper, green beans, broccoli and cauliflower. Transfer to a Chinese sand pot or earthenware casserole. Cover and place towards the bottom of the oven.

7 Stir the tofu and marinade, then place the dish on a shelf near the top of the oven. Cook for 30 minutes. Remove both the dish and the sand pot or casserole from the oven. Add the tofu, with any remaining marinade, to the curry, with the mushrooms, and stir well.

8 Return the sand pot or casserole to the oven, reduce the temperature to 180°C/350°F/Gas 4 and cook for about 15 minutes, or until the vegetables are tender. Garnish with the spring onions and serve with the rice or noodles.

COOK'S TIP
Tofu or beancurd is made from soya beans and is sold in blocks. It is a creamy white colour and has a solid gel-like texture. Tofu has a bland flavour and its absorbent nature means that it takes on the flavours of marinades or other foods with which it is cooked.

SWEET PUMPKIN AND PEANUT CURRY

A HEARTY, SOOTHING CURRY PERFECT FOR AUTUMN OR WINTER EVENINGS. ITS CHEERFUL COLOUR ALONE WILL BRIGHTEN YOU UP — AND IT TASTES TERRIFIC.

SERVES FOUR

INGREDIENTS

30ml/2 tbsp vegetable oil
4 garlic cloves, crushed
4 shallots, finely chopped
30ml/2 tbsp yellow curry paste
600ml/1 pint/2½ cups
　vegetable stock
2 kaffir lime leaves, torn
15ml/1 tbsp chopped fresh galangal
450g/1lb pumpkin, peeled, seeded
　and diced
225g/8oz sweet potatoes, diced
90g/3½oz/scant 1 cup peanuts,
　roasted and chopped
300ml/½ pint/1¼ cups coconut milk
90g/3½oz/1½ cups chestnut
　mushrooms, sliced
15ml/1 tbsp soy sauce
30ml/2 tbsp Thai fish sauce
50g/2oz/⅓ cup pumpkin
　seeds, toasted, and fresh green
　chilli flowers, to garnish

1 Heat the oil in a large pan. Add the garlic and shallots and cook over a medium heat, stirring occasionally, for 10 minutes, until softened and golden. Do not let them burn.

2 Add the yellow curry paste and stir-fry over a medium heat for 30 seconds, until fragrant, then add the stock, lime leaves, galangal, pumpkin and sweet potatoes. Bring to the boil, stirring frequently, then reduce the heat to low and simmer gently for 15 minutes.

3 Add the peanuts, coconut milk and mushrooms. Stir in the soy sauce and fish sauce and simmer for 5 minutes more. Spoon into warmed individual serving bowls, garnish with the pumpkin seeds and chillies and serve.

COOK'S TIP
The well-drained vegetables from any of these curries would make a very tasty filling for a pastry or pie. This may not be a Thai tradition, but it is a good example of fusion food.

CORN AND CASHEW NUT CURRY

A SUBSTANTIAL CURRY, THIS COMBINES ALL THE ESSENTIAL FLAVOURS OF SOUTHERN THAILAND. IT IS DELICIOUSLY AROMATIC, BUT THE FLAVOUR IS FAIRLY MILD.

SERVES FOUR

INGREDIENTS
30ml/2 tbsp vegetable oil
4 shallots, chopped
90g/3½oz/scant 1 cup cashew nuts
5ml/1 tsp Thai red curry paste
400g/14oz potatoes, peeled and cut into chunks
1 lemon grass stalk, finely chopped
200g/7oz can chopped tomatoes
600ml/1 pint/2½ cups boiling water
200g/7oz/generous 1 cup drained canned whole kernel corn
4 celery sticks, sliced
2 kaffir lime leaves, rolled into cylinders and thinly sliced
15ml/1 tbsp tomato ketchup
15ml/1 tbsp light soy sauce
5ml/1 tsp palm sugar or light muscovado (brown) sugar
5ml/1 tsp Thai fish sauce
4 spring onions (scallions), thinly sliced
small bunch fresh basil, chopped

COOK'S TIP
Rolling the lime leaves into cylinders before slicing produces very fine strips – a technique known as cutting *en chiffonnade*. Remove the central rib from the leaves before cutting them.

1 Heat the oil in a large, heavy pan or wok. Add the shallots and stir-fry over a medium heat for 2–3 minutes, until softened. Add the cashew nuts and stir-fry for a few minutes until golden.

2 Stir in the red curry paste. Stir-fry for 1 minute, then add the potatoes, lemon grass, tomatoes and boiling water.

3 Bring back to the boil, then reduce the heat to low, cover and simmer gently for 15–20 minutes, or until the potatoes are tender.

4 Stir the corn, celery, lime leaves, tomato ketchup, soy sauce, sugar and fish sauce into the pan or wok. Simmer for a further 5 minutes, until heated through, then spoon into warmed serving bowls. Sprinkle with the sliced spring onions and basil and serve.

AUBERGINE AND SWEET POTATO STEW WITH COCONUT MILK

SCENTED WITH FRAGRANT LEMON GRASS, GINGER AND LOTS OF GARLIC, THIS IS A PARTICULARLY GOOD COMBINATION OF FLAVOURS. AUBERGINES AND SWEET POTATOES GO WELL TOGETHER AND THE COCONUT MILK ADDS A MELLOW NOTE.

SERVES SIX

INGREDIENTS

  400g/14oz baby aubergines
    (eggplants) or 2 standard aubergines
  60ml/4 tbsp groundnut (peanut) oil
  225g/8oz Thai red shallots or other
    small shallots or pickling onions
  5ml/1 tsp fennel seeds,
    lightly crushed
  4–5 garlic cloves, thinly sliced
  25ml/1½ tbsp finely chopped fresh
    root ginger
  475ml/16fl oz/2 cups vegetable stock
  2 lemon grass stalks, outer layers
    discarded, finely chopped or minced
  15g/½oz/⅔ cup fresh coriander
    (cilantro), stalks and leaves
    chopped separately
  3 kaffir lime leaves, lightly bruised
  2–3 small fresh red chillies
  45–60ml/3–4 tbsp Thai green
    curry paste
  675g/1½lb sweet potatoes, peeled
    and cut into thick chunks
  400ml/14fl oz/1⅔ cups coconut milk
  2.5–5ml/½–1 tsp palm sugar or light
    muscovado (brown) sugar
  250g/9oz/3½ cups mushrooms,
    thickly sliced
  juice of 1 lime, to taste
  salt and ground black pepper
  boiled rice and 18 fresh Thai basil
    or ordinary basil leaves, to serve

1 Trim the aubergines. Slice baby aubergines in half lengthways. Cut standard aubergines into chunks.

2 Heat half the oil in a wide pan or deep, lidded frying pan. Add the aubergines and cook (uncovered) over a medium heat, stirring occasionally, until lightly browned on all sides. Remove from the pan and set aside.

3 Slice 4–5 of the shallots. Cook the whole shallots in the oil remaining in the pan, adding a little more oil if necessary, until lightly browned. Set aside with the aubergines. Add the remaining oil to the pan and cook the sliced shallots, fennel seeds, garlic and ginger over a low heat for 5 minutes.

4 Pour in the vegetable stock, then add the lemon grass, chopped coriander stalks and any roots, lime leaves and whole chillies. Cover and simmer over a low heat for 5 minutes.

5 Stir in 30ml/2 tbsp of the curry paste and the sweet potatoes. Simmer gently for about 10 minutes, then return the aubergines and browned shallots to the pan and cook for a further 5 minutes.

6 Stir in the coconut milk and the sugar. Season to taste with salt and pepper, then stir in the mushrooms and simmer gently for 5 minutes, or until all the vegetables are cooked and tender.

7 Stir in more curry paste and lime juice to taste, followed by the chopped coriander leaves. Adjust the seasoning, if necessary, and ladle the vegetables into warmed bowls. Sprinkle basil leaves over the stew and serve with rice.

COOK'S TIP
Although this is called a stew, green curry paste is an important ingredient, as it is in most of these recipes. The quantity given is only a guide, however, so use less if you prefer.

SNAKE BEANS WITH TOFU

ANOTHER NAME FOR SNAKE BEANS IS YARD-LONG BEANS. THIS IS SOMETHING OF AN EXAGGERATION BUT THEY DO GROW TO LENGTHS OF 35CM/14IN AND MORE. LOOK FOR THEM IN ASIAN STORES AND MARKETS, BUT IF YOU CAN'T FIND ANY, SUBSTITUTE OTHER GREEN BEANS.

SERVES FOUR

INGREDIENTS

- 500g/1¼lb long beans, thinly sliced
- 200g/7oz silken tofu, cut into cubes
- 2 shallots, thinly sliced
- 200ml/7fl oz/scant 1 cup coconut milk
- 115g/4oz/1 cup roasted peanuts, chopped
- juice of 1 lime
- 10ml/2 tsp palm sugar or light muscovado (brown) sugar
- 60ml/4 tbsp soy sauce
- 5ml/1 tsp dried chilli flakes

VARIATIONS

The sauce also works very well with mangetouts (snow peas). Alternatively, stir in sliced yellow or red (bell) pepper.

1 Bring a pan of lightly salted water to the boil. Add the beans and blanch them for 30 seconds.

2 Drain the beans immediately, then refresh under cold water and drain again, shaking well to remove as much water as possible. Place in a serving bowl and set aside.

3 Put the tofu and shallots in a pan with the coconut milk. Heat gently, stirring, until the tofu begins to crumble.

4 Add the peanuts, lime juice, sugar, soy sauce and chilli flakes. Heat, stirring, until the sugar has dissolved. Pour the sauce over the beans, toss to combine and serve immediately.

MUSHROOMS <u>WITH</u> GARLIC <u>AND</u> CHILLI SAUCE

When you are planning a barbecue for friends and family, it can be tricky finding something really special for the vegetarians in the party. These tasty mushroom kebabs are ideal because they look, smell and taste wonderful.

SERVES FOUR

INGREDIENTS

   12 large field (portabello), chestnut
     or oyster mushrooms or a mixture,
     cut in half
   4 garlic cloves, coarsely
     chopped
   6 coriander (cilantro) roots,
     coarsely chopped
   15ml/1 tbsp granulated sugar
   30ml/2 tbsp light soy sauce
   ground black pepper
For the dipping sauce
   15ml/1 tbsp granulated sugar
   90ml/6 tbsp rice vinegar
   5ml/1 tsp salt
   1 garlic clove, crushed
   1 small fresh red chilli, seeded
     and finely chopped

1 If using wooden skewers, soak eight of them in cold water for at least 30 minutes to prevent them burning over the barbecue or under the grill.

2 Make the dipping sauce by heating the sugar, rice vinegar and salt in a small pan, stirring occasionally until the sugar and salt have dissolved. Add the garlic and chilli, pour into a serving dish and keep warm.

3 Thread three mushroom halves on to each skewer. Lay the filled skewers side by side in a shallow dish.

4 In a mortar or spice grinder pound or blend the garlic and coriander roots. Scrape into a bowl and mix with the sugar, soy sauce and a little pepper.

5 Brush the soy sauce mixture over the mushrooms and leave to marinate for 15 minutes. Prepare the barbecue or preheat the grill (broiler) and cook the mushrooms for 2–3 minutes on each side. Serve with the dipping sauce.

STUFFED SWEET PEPPERS

*THIS IS AN UNUSUAL RECIPE IN THAT THE STUFFED PEPPERS ARE STEAMED RATHER THAN BAKED,
BUT THE RESULT IS BEAUTIFULLY LIGHT AND TENDER. THE FILLING INCORPORATES TYPICAL THAI
INGREDIENTS SUCH AS RED CURRY PASTE AND FISH SAUCE.*

SERVES FOUR

INGREDIENTS

   3 garlic cloves, finely chopped
   2 coriander (cilantro) roots,
    finely chopped
  400g/14oz/3 cups
    mushrooms, quartered
  5ml/1 tsp Thai red curry paste
  1 egg, lightly beaten
  15ml/1 tbsp Thai fish sauce
  15ml/1 tbsp light soy sauce
  2.5ml/½ tsp granulated sugar
  3 kaffir lime leaves, finely chopped
  4 yellow (bell) peppers, halved
    lengthways and seeded

VARIATIONS
Use red or orange (bell) peppers if you
prefer, or a combination of the two.

1 In a mortar or spice grinder pound or
blend the garlic with the coriander
roots. Scrape into a bowl.

2 Put the mushrooms in a food
processor and pulse briefly until they
are finely chopped. Add to the garlic
mixture, then stir in the curry paste,
egg, sauces, sugar and lime leaves.

3 Place the pepper halves in a single
layer in a steamer basket. Spoon the
mixture loosely into the pepper halves.
Do not pack the mixture down tightly
or the filling will dry out too much.
Bring the water in the steamer to the
boil, then lower the heat to a simmer.
Steam the peppers for 15 minutes, or
until the flesh is tender. Serve hot.

SWEET AND SOUR VEGETABLES WITH TOFU

BIG, BOLD AND BEAUTIFUL, THIS IS A HEARTY STIR-FRY THAT WILL SATISFY THE HUNGRIEST GUESTS. STIR-FRIES ARE ALWAYS A GOOD CHOICE WHEN ENTERTAINING AS YOU CAN PREPARE THE INGREDIENTS AHEAD OF TIME AND THEN THEY TAKE SUCH A SHORT TIME TO COOK.

SERVES FOUR

INGREDIENTS
4 shallots
3 garlic cloves
30ml/2 tbsp groundnut (peanut) oil
250g/9oz Chinese leaves (Chinese cabbage), shredded
8 baby corn cobs, sliced on the diagonal
2 red (bell) peppers, seeded and thinly sliced
200g/7oz/1¾ cups mangetouts (snow peas), trimmed and sliced
250g/9oz tofu, rinsed, drained and cut in 1cm/½in cubes
60ml/4 tbsp vegetable stock
30ml/2 tbsp light soy sauce
15ml/1 tbsp granulated sugar
30ml/2 tbsp rice vinegar
2.5ml/½ tsp dried chilli flakes
small bunch coriander (cilantro), chopped

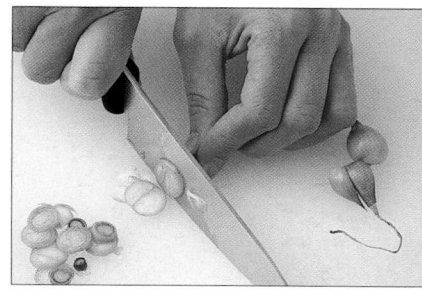

1 Slice the shallots thinly using a sharp knife. Finely chop the garlic.

2 Heat the oil in a wok or large frying pan and cook the shallots and garlic for 2–3 minutes over a medium heat, until golden. Do not let the garlic burn or it will taste bitter.

3 Add the shredded cabbage, toss over the heat for 30 seconds, then add the corn cobs and repeat the process.

4 Add the red peppers, mangetouts and tofu in the same way, each time adding a single ingredient and tossing it over the heat for about 30 seconds before adding the next ingredient.

5 Pour in the stock and soy sauce. Mix together the sugar and vinegar in a small bowl, stirring until the sugar has dissolved, then add to the wok or pan. Sprinkle over the chilli flakes and coriander, toss to mix well and serve.

FISH AND SHELLFISH

You need only glance at a map to discover why Thailand has so many wonderful fish and shellfish dishes. The country has a long coastline, most of it on the fish-rich Gulf of Siam, and major rivers provide a wide variety of freshwater fish. Prawns and shrimp are very popular, not just fresh, but also dried. All kinds of seafood go well with the classic Thai combinations of subtle flavourings, especially the sharp elements provided by limes, kaffir lime leaves, lemon grass and tamarind.

SWEET AND SOUR FISH

WHEN FISH SUCH AS RED MULLET OR SNAPPER IS COOKED IN THIS WAY THE SKIN BECOMES CRISP, WHILE THE FLESH INSIDE REMAINS MOIST AND JUICY. THE SWEET AND SOUR SAUCE, WITH ITS COLOURFUL CHERRY TOMATOES, COMPLEMENTS THE FISH BEAUTIFULLY.

SERVES FOUR TO SIX

INGREDIENTS

1 large or 2 medium fish, such as
    snapper or mullet, heads removed
20ml/4 tsp cornflour (cornstarch)
120ml/4fl oz/½ cup vegetable oil
15ml/1 tbsp chopped garlic
15ml/1 tbsp chopped fresh
    root ginger
30ml/2 tbsp chopped shallots
225g/8oz cherry tomatoes
30ml/2 tbsp red wine vinegar
30ml/2 tbsp granulated sugar
30ml/2 tbsp tomato ketchup
15ml/1 tbsp Thai fish sauce
45ml/3 tbsp water
salt and ground black pepper
coriander (cilantro) leaves and
    shredded spring onions
    (scallions), to garnish

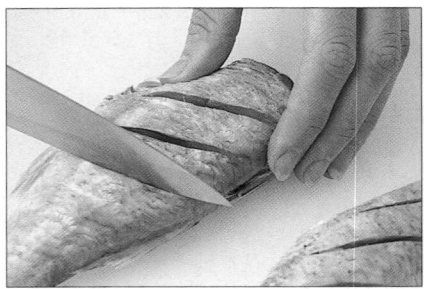

1 Rinse and dry the fish. Score the skin diagonally on both sides, then coat the fish lightly all over with 15ml/1 tbsp of the cornflour. Shake off any excess.

2 Heat the oil in a wok or large frying pan. Add the fish and cook over a medium heat for 6–7 minutes. Turn the fish over and cook for 6–7 minutes more, until it is crisp and brown.

3 Remove the fish with a metal spatula or fish slice and place on a large platter. Pour off all but 30ml/2 tbsp of the oil from the wok or pan and reheat. Add the garlic, ginger and shallots and cook over a medium heat, stirring occasionally, for 3–4 minutes, until golden.

4 Add the cherry tomatoes and cook until they burst open. Stir in the vinegar, sugar, tomato ketchup and fish sauce. Lower the heat and simmer gently for 1–2 minutes, then taste and adjust the seasoning, adding more vinegar, sugar and/or fish sauce, if necessary.

5 In a cup, mix the remaining 5ml/1 tsp cornflour to a paste with the water. Stir into the sauce. Heat, stirring, until it thickens. Pour the sauce over the fish, garnish with coriander leaves and shredded spring onions and serve.

STEAMED FISH WITH CHILLI SAUCE

STEAMING IS ONE OF THE BEST METHODS OF COOKING FISH. BY LEAVING THE FISH WHOLE AND ON THE BONE, MAXIMUM FLAVOUR IS RETAINED AND THE FLESH REMAINS BEAUTIFULLY MOIST. THE BANANA LEAF IS BOTH AUTHENTIC AND ATTRACTIVE, BUT YOU CAN USE BAKING PARCHMENT.

SERVES FOUR

INGREDIENTS

   1 large or 2 medium firm fish such
     as sea bass or grouper, scaled
     and cleaned
   30ml/2 tbsp rice wine
   3 fresh red chillies, seeded and
     thinly sliced
   2 garlic cloves, finely chopped
   2cm/¾in piece fresh root ginger,
     peeled and finely shredded
   2 lemon grass stalks, crushed and
     finely chopped
   2 spring onions
     (scallions), chopped
   30ml/2 tbsp Thai fish sauce
   juice of 1 lime
   1 fresh banana leaf
For the chilli sauce
   10 fresh red chillies, seeded
     and chopped
   4 garlic cloves, chopped
   60ml/4 tbsp Thai fish sauce
   15ml/1 tbsp granulated sugar
   75ml/5 tbsp fresh lime juice

1 Thoroughly rinse the fish under cold running water. Pat it dry with kitchen paper. With a sharp knife, slash the skin of the fish a few times on both sides.

2 Mix together the rice wine, chillies, garlic, shredded ginger, lemon grass and spring onions in a non-metallic bowl. Add the fish sauce and lime juice and mix to a paste. Place the fish on the banana leaf and spread the spice paste evenly over it, rubbing it in well where the skin has been slashed.

3 Put a rack or a small upturned plate in the base of a wok. Pour in boiling water to a depth of 5cm/2in. Lift the banana leaf, together with the fish, and place it on the rack or plate. Cover with a lid and steam for 10–15 minutes, or until the fish is cooked.

4 Meanwhile, make the sauce. Place all the ingredients in a food processor and process until smooth. If the mixture seems to be too thick, add a little cold water. Scrape into a serving bowl.

5 Serve the fish hot, on the banana leaf if you like, with the sweet chilli sauce to spoon over the top.

HOT AND FRAGRANT TROUT

THIS WICKEDLY HOT SPICE PASTE COULD BE USED AS A MARINADE FOR ANY FISH OR MEAT. IT ALSO MAKES A WONDERFUL SPICY DIP FOR GRILLED MEAT.

SERVES FOUR

INGREDIENTS

    2 large fresh green chillies, seeded
      and coarsely chopped
    5 shallots, peeled
    5 garlic cloves, peeled
    30ml/2 tbsp fresh lime juice
    30ml/2 tbsp Thai fish sauce
    15ml/1 tbsp palm sugar or light
      muscovado (brown) sugar
    4 kaffir lime leaves, rolled
      into cylinders and
      thinly sliced
    2 trout or similar firm-fleshed
      fish, about 350g/12oz
      each, cleaned
    fresh garlic chives, to garnish
    boiled rice, to serve

1 Wrap the chillies, shallots and garlic in a foil package. Place under a hot grill (broiler) for 10 minutes, until softened.

2 When the package is cool enough to handle, place the contents in a mortar or food processor and pound with a pestle or process to a paste.

3 Add the lime juice, fish sauce, sugar and lime leaves and mix well. With a teaspoon, stuff this paste inside the fish. Smear a little on the skin too. Grill (broil) the fish for about 5 minutes on each side, until just cooked through. Lift the fish on to a platter, garnish with garlic chives and serve with rice.

TROUT WITH TAMARIND AND CHILLI SAUCE

SOMETIMES TROUT CAN TASTE RATHER BLAND, BUT THIS SPICY SAUCE REALLY GIVES IT A ZING. IF YOU LIKE YOUR FOOD VERY SPICY, ADD AN EXTRA CHILLI.

SERVES FOUR

INGREDIENTS
    4 trout, cleaned
    6 spring onions (scallions), sliced
    60ml/4 tbsp soy sauce
    15ml/1 tbsp vegetable oil
    30ml/2 tbsp chopped fresh coriander
      (cilantro) and strips of fresh red
      chilli, to garnish
For the sauce
    50g/2oz tamarind pulp
    105ml/7 tbsp boiling water
    2 shallots, coarsely chopped
    1 fresh red chilli, seeded and chopped
    1cm/½in piece fresh root ginger,
      peeled and chopped
    5ml/1 tsp soft light brown sugar
    45ml/3 tbsp Thai fish sauce

3 Make the sauce. Put the tamarind pulp in a small bowl and pour on the boiling water. Mash well with a fork until softened. Transfer the tamarind mixture to a food processor or blender, and add the shallots, fresh chilli, ginger, sugar and fish sauce. Process to a coarse pulp. Scrape into a bowl.

4 Heat the oil in a large frying pan or wok and cook the trout, one at a time if necessary, for about 5 minutes on each side, until the skin is crisp and browned and the flesh cooked. Put on warmed plates and spoon over some of the sauce. Sprinkle with the coriander and chilli and serve with the remaining sauce.

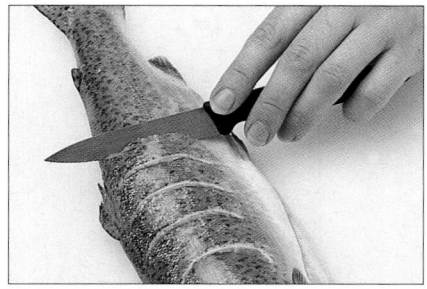

1 Slash the trout diagonally four or five times on each side. Place them in a shallow dish that is large enough to hold them all in a single layer.

2 Fill the cavities with spring onions and douse each fish with soy sauce. Carefully turn the fish over to coat both sides with the sauce. Sprinkle any remaining spring onions over the top.

NORTHERN FISH CURRY <u>WITH</u> SHALLOTS <u>AND</u> LEMON GRASS

THIS IS A THIN, SOUPY CURRY WITH WONDERFULLY STRONG FLAVOURS. SERVE IT IN BOWLS WITH LOTS OF STICKY RICE TO SOAK UP THE DELICIOUS JUICES.

SERVES FOUR

INGREDIENTS

450g/1lb salmon fillet
500ml/17fl oz/2¼ cups
   vegetable stock
4 shallots, finely chopped
2 garlic cloves, finely chopped
2.5cm/1in piece fresh galangal,
   finely chopped
1 lemon grass stalk, finely chopped
2.5ml/½ tsp dried chilli flakes
15ml/1 tbsp Thai fish sauce
5ml/1 tsp palm sugar or light
   muscovado (brown) sugar

1 Place the salmon in the freezer for 30–40 minutes to firm up the flesh slightly. Remove and discard the skin, then use a sharp knife to cut the fish into 2.5cm/1in cubes, removing any stray bones with your fingers or with tweezers as you do so.

2 Pour the stock into a large, heavy pan and bring it to the boil over a medium heat. Add the shallots, garlic, galangal, lemon grass, chilli flakes, fish sauce and sugar. Bring back to the boil, stir well, then reduce the heat and simmer gently for 15 minutes.

3 Add the fish, bring back to the boil, then turn off the heat. Leave the curry to stand for 10–15 minutes until the fish is cooked through, then serve.

STIR-FRIED PRAWNS <u>WITH</u> TAMARIND

THE SOUR, TANGY FLAVOUR THAT IS CHARACTERISTIC OF MANY THAI DISHES COMES FROM FRESH TAMARIND PODS, WHICH COME FROM THE TAMARIND TREE. YOU CAN BUY FRESH PODS, BUT PREPARING THEM FOR COOKING IS A LABORIOUS PROCESS, AND ITS MUCH EASIER TO USE A BLOCK OF PASTE.

SERVES FOUR TO SIX

INGREDIENTS
  6 dried red chillies
  30ml/2 tbsp vegetable oil
  30ml/2 tbsp chopped onion
  30ml/2 tbsp palm sugar or light
    muscovado (brown) sugar
  30ml/2 tbsp chicken stock or water
  15ml/1 tbsp Thai fish sauce
  90ml/6 tbsp tamarind juice, made
    by mixing tamarind paste with
    warm water
  450g/1lb raw prawns
    (shrimp), peeled
  15ml/1 tbsp fried chopped garlic
  30ml/2 tbsp fried sliced shallots
  2 spring onions (scallions), chopped,
    to garnish

1 Heat a wok or large frying pan, but do not add any oil at this stage. Add the dried chillies and dry-fry them by pressing them against the surface of the wok or pan with a spatula, turning them occasionally. Do not let them burn. Set them aside to cool slightly.

2 Add the oil to the wok or pan and reheat. Add the chopped onion and cook over a medium heat, stirring occasionally, for 2–3 minutes, until softened and golden brown.

3 Add the sugar, stock or water, fish sauce, dry-fried red chillies and the tamarind juice, stirring constantly until the sugar has dissolved. Bring to the boil, then lower the heat slightly.

4 Add the prawns, garlic and shallots. Toss over the heat for 3–4 minutes, until the prawns are cooked. Garnish with the spring onions and serve.

COOK'S TIP
Leave a few prawns (shrimp) in their shells for a garnish, if you like.

SATAY PRAWNS

THIS DELICIOUS DISH IS INSPIRED BY THE CLASSIC INDONESIAN SATAY. THE COMBINATION OF MILD PEANUTS, AROMATIC SPICES, SWEET COCONUT MILK AND ZESTY LEMON JUICE IN THE SPICY DIP IS PERFECT AND IS GUARANTEED TO HAVE GUESTS COMING BACK FOR MORE.

SERVES FOUR TO SIX

INGREDIENTS
   450g/1lb king prawns (jumbo shrimp)
   25ml/1½ tbsp vegetable oil
For the peanut sauce
   25ml/1½ tbsp vegetable oil
   15ml/1 tbsp chopped garlic
   1 small onion, chopped
   3–4 fresh red chillies, seeded
     and chopped
   3 kaffir lime leaves, torn
   1 lemon grass stalk, bruised
     and chopped
   5ml/1 tsp medium curry paste
   250ml/8fl oz/1 cup coconut milk
   1cm/½in piece cinnamon stick
   75g/3oz/⅓ cup crunchy
     peanut butter
   45ml/3 tbsp tamarind juice, made
     by mixing tamarind paste with
     warm water
   30ml/2 tbsp Thai fish sauce
   30ml/2 tbsp palm sugar or light
     muscovado (brown) sugar
   juice of ½ lemon
For the garnish
   ½ bunch fresh coriander
     (cilantro) leaves (optional)
   4 fresh red chillies, finely sliced
     (optional)
   spring onions (scallions),
     cut diagonally

1 Remove the heads from the prawns and peel, leaving the tail ends intact. Slit each prawn along the back with a small, sharp knife and remove the black vein. Rinse under cold running water, pat completely dry on kitchen paper and set the prawns aside.

2 Make the peanut sauce. Heat half the oil in a wok or large, heavy frying pan. Add the garlic and onion and cook over a medium heat, stirring occasionally, for 3–4 minutes, until the mixture has softened but not browned.

3 Add the chillies, kaffir lime leaves, lemon grass and curry paste. Stir well and cook for a further 2–3 minutes, then stir in the coconut milk, cinnamon stick, peanut butter, tamarind juice, fish sauce, sugar and lemon juice. Cook, stirring constantly, until well blended.

4 Bring to the boil, then reduce the heat to low and simmer gently for 15–20 minutes, until the sauce thickens. Stir occasionally with a wooden spoon to prevent the sauce from sticking to the base of the wok or frying pan.

5 Thread the prawns on to skewers and brush with a little oil. Cook under a preheated grill (broiler) for 2 minutes on each side until they turn pink and are firm to the touch. Alternatively, pan-fry the prawns, then thread on to skewers.

6 Remove the cinnamon stick from the sauce and discard. Arrange the skewered prawns on a warmed platter, garnish with spring onions and coriander leaves and sliced red chillies, if liked, and serve with the sauce.

VARIATIONS
• For a curry-style dish, heat the oil in a wok or large frying pan. Add the prawns (shrimp) and stir-fry for 3–4 minutes, or until pink. Mix the prawns with the sauce and serve with jasmine rice.
• You can use this basic sauce for satay pork or chicken, too. With a sharp knife, cut pork fillet (tenderloin) or skinless, boneless chicken breast portions into long thin strips and stir-fry in hot oil until golden brown all over and cooked through. Then stir into the sauce instead of the king prawns (jumbo shrimp).
• You could use Thai red or green curry paste for this recipe. Make your own or buy a good-quality product from an Asian food store. Once opened, jars of curry paste should be kept in the refrigerator and used within 2 months.
• You can make the satay sauce in advance and leave it to cool. Transfer to a bowl, cover with clear film (plastic wrap) and store in the refrigerator. Reheat gently, stirring occasionally, before stir-frying the prawns (shrimp).

PAN-STEAMED MUSSELS <u>WITH</u> THAI HERBS

LIKE SO MANY THAI DISHES, THIS IS VERY EASY TO PREPARE. THE LEMON GRASS AND KAFFIR LIME LEAVES ADD A REFRESHING TANG TO THE MUSSELS.

SERVES FOUR TO SIX

INGREDIENTS

1kg/2¼lb fresh mussels
2 lemon grass stalks, finely chopped
4 shallots, chopped
4 kaffir lime leaves, coarsely torn
2 fresh red chillies, sliced
15ml/1 tbsp Thai fish sauce
30ml/2 tbsp fresh lime juice
thinly sliced spring onions (scallions)
  and coriander (cilantro) leaves,
  to garnish

1 Clean the mussels by pulling off the beards, scrubbing the shells well and removing any barnacles. Discard any mussels that are broken or which do not close when tapped sharply.

2 Place the mussels in a large, heavy pan and add the lemon grass, shallots, kaffir lime leaves, chillies, fish sauce and lime juice. Mix well. Cover the pan tightly and steam the mussels over a high heat, shaking the pan occasionally, for 5–7 minutes, until the shells have opened.

3 Using a slotted spoon, transfer the cooked mussels to a warmed serving dish or individual bowls. Discard any mussels that have failed to open.

4 Garnish the mussels with the thinly sliced spring onions and coriander leaves. Serve immediately.

CRAB <u>AND</u> TOFU STIR-FRY

FOR A YEAR-ROUND LIGHT MEAL, THIS SPEEDY STIR-FRY IS THE IDEAL CHOICE. AS YOU NEED ONLY A LITTLE CRAB MEAT — AND YOU COULD USE THE CANNED VARIETY — THIS IS A VERY ECONOMICAL DISH.

SERVES TWO

INGREDIENTS
  250g/9oz silken tofu
  60ml/4 tbsp vegetable oil
  2 garlic cloves, finely chopped
  115g/4oz white crab meat
  130g/4½oz/generous 1 cup baby
    corn, halved lengthways
  2 spring onions (scallions), chopped
  1 fresh red chilli, seeded and
    finely chopped
  30ml/2 tbsp soy sauce
  15ml/1 tbsp Thai fish sauce
  5ml/1 tsp palm sugar or light
    muscovado (brown) sugar
  juice of 1 lime
  small bunch fresh coriander
    (cilantro), chopped, to garnish

1 Using a sharp knife, cut the silken tofu into 1cm/½in cubes.

2 Heat the oil in a wok or large, heavy frying pan. Add the tofu cubes and stir-fry until golden all over, taking care not to break them up. Remove the tofu with a slotted spoon and set aside.

3 Add the garlic to the wok or pan and stir-fry until golden. Add the crab meat, tofu, corn, spring onions, chilli, soy sauce, fish sauce and sugar. Cook, stirring constantly, until the vegetables are just tender. Stir in the lime juice, transfer to warmed bowls, sprinkle with the coriander and serve immediately.

POULTRY
AND MEAT

Chicken and pork have long been popular in Thailand, and beef has more recently come into favour too, while Chinese influence has brought duck into Thai dishes. Poultry and meats are often marinated in hot and fragrant spices, allowing the complex flavours to develop, and can be simply roasted (traditionally on a spit, but an oven works just as well), stir-fried, or cooked on a barbecue — always a popular choice.

RED CHICKEN CURRY WITH BAMBOO SHOOTS

BAMBOO SHOOTS HAVE A LOVELY CRUNCHY TEXTURE. IT IS QUITE ACCEPTABLE TO USE CANNED ONES, AS FRESH BAMBOO IS NOT READILY AVAILABLE IN THE WEST. BUY CANNED WHOLE BAMBOO SHOOTS, WHICH ARE CRISPER AND OF BETTER QUALITY THAN SLICED SHOOTS.

SERVES FOUR TO SIX

INGREDIENTS

1 litre/1¾ pints/4 cups coconut milk
450g/1lb skinless, boneless chicken
 breast portions, diced
30ml/2 tbsp Thai fish sauce
15ml/1 tbsp granulated sugar
1–2 drained canned bamboo shoots,
 total weight about 225g/8oz, rinsed
 and sliced
5 kaffir lime leaves, torn
salt and ground black pepper
chopped fresh red chillies and kaffir
 lime leaves, to garnish
For the red curry paste
 5ml/1 tsp coriander seeds
 2.5ml/½ tsp cumin seeds
 12–15 fresh red chillies, seeded and
  coarsely chopped
 4 shallots, thinly sliced
 2 garlic cloves, chopped
 15ml/1 tbsp chopped
  fresh galangal
 2 lemon grass stalks, chopped
 3 kaffir lime leaves, chopped
 4 fresh coriander (cilantro) roots
 10 black peppercorns
 good pinch ground cinnamon
 5ml/1 tsp ground turmeric
 2.5ml/½ tsp shrimp paste
 5ml/1 tsp salt
 30ml/2 tbsp vegetable oil

2 Add the vegetable oil, a little at a time, mixing or processing well after each addition. Transfer to a screw-top jar, put on the lid and keep in the refrigerator until ready to use.

3 Pour half of the coconut milk into a large, heavy pan. Bring to the boil over a medium heat, stirring constantly until the coconut milk has separated.

4 Stir in 30ml/2 tbsp of the red curry paste and cook the mixture, stirring constantly, for 2–3 minutes, until the curry paste is thoroughly incorporated. The remaining red curry paste can be kept in the closed jar in the refrigerator for up to 3 months.

5 Add the diced chicken, fish sauce and sugar to the pan. Stir well, then lower the heat and cook gently for 5–6 minutes, stirring until the chicken changes colour and is cooked through. Take care that the curry does not stick to the base of the pan.

6 Pour the remaining coconut milk into the pan, then add the sliced bamboo shoots and torn lime leaves. Bring back to the boil over a medium heat, stirring constantly to prevent the mixture from sticking to the pan, then taste and add salt and pepper if necessary.

7 To serve, spoon the curry into a warmed serving dish and garnish with the chopped chillies and lime leaves.

VARIATION
Instead of, or as well as, bamboo shoots, use straw mushrooms. Fresh straw mushrooms are not often seen in the West, but they are available in cans from Asian stores and supermarkets. Drain well and stir into the curry at the end of the recipe. Straw mushrooms are prized for their slippery texture as well as for their delicate, but delicious flavour.

COOK'S TIP
It is essential to use chicken breast portions, rather than any other cut, for this curry, as it is cooked very quickly. To save time, rather than cutting whole portions into bitesize pieces yourself, look for diced chicken or strips of chicken (which are frequently labelled "stir-fry chicken") in the supermarket.

1 Make the curry paste. Dry-fry the coriander seeds and cumin seeds for 1–2 minutes, then put in a mortar or food processor with all the remaining ingredients except the oil. Pound or process to a paste.

BARBECUE CHICKEN

CHICKEN COOKED ON A BARBECUE IS SERVED ALMOST EVERYWHERE IN THAILAND, FROM ROADSIDE STALLS TO SPORTS STADIA. THIS IS THE PERFECT DISH FOR A SUMMER PARTY, BUT YOU CAN ALSO COOK THIS TASTY CHICKEN IN THE OVEN IF THE WEATHER PROVES DISAPPOINTING.

SERVES FOUR TO SIX

INGREDIENTS
    1 chicken, about 1.5kg/3–3½lb, cut
        into 8–10 pieces
    lime wedges and fresh red chillies,
        to garnish
For the marinade
    2 lemon grass stalks, roots trimmed
    2.5cm/1in piece fresh root ginger,
        peeled and thinly sliced
    6 garlic cloves, coarsely chopped
    4 shallots, coarsely chopped
    ½ bunch coriander (cilantro)
        roots, chopped
    15ml/1 tbsp palm sugar or light
        muscovado (brown) sugar
    120ml/4fl oz/½ cup coconut milk
    30ml/2 tbsp Thai fish sauce
    30ml/2 tbsp light soy sauce

1 Make the marinade. Cut off the lower 5cm/2in of the lemon grass stalks and chop them coarsely. Put into a food processor with the ginger, garlic, shallots, coriander, sugar, coconut milk and sauces and process until smooth.

2 Place the chicken pieces in a dish, pour over the marinade and stir to mix well. Cover the dish and leave in a cool place to marinate for at least 4 hours, or leave it in the refrigerator overnight.

3 Prepare the barbecue or preheat the oven to 200°C/400°F/Gas 6. Drain the chicken, reserving the marinade. If you are cooking in the oven, arrange the chicken pieces in a single layer on a rack set over a roasting pan.

4 Cook the chicken on the barbecue over moderately hot coals or on medium heat for a gas barbecue, or bake in the oven for 20–30 minutes. Turn the pieces and brush with the reserved marinade once or twice during cooking.

5 As soon as the chicken pieces are golden brown and cooked through, transfer them to a serving platter, garnish with the lime wedges and red chillies and serve immediately.

COOK'S TIPS
• Coconut milk is available fresh or in cans or cartons from Asian food stores and most supermarkets and you may also find it in powdered form. Alternatively, use 50g/2oz creamed coconut from a packet and stir it into warm water until completely dissolved.
• Coriander roots are more intensely flavoured than the leaves, but the herb is not always available with the roots intact.

FRAGRANT GRILLED CHICKEN

IF YOU HAVE TIME, PREPARE THE CHICKEN IN ADVANCE AND LEAVE IT TO MARINATE IN THE REFRIGERATOR FOR SEVERAL HOURS — OR EVEN OVERNIGHT — UNTIL READY TO COOK.

SERVES FOUR

INGREDIENTS

450g/1lb boneless chicken breast
portions, with the skin on
30ml/2 tbsp sesame oil
2 garlic cloves, crushed
2 coriander (cilantro) roots,
finely chopped
2 small fresh red chillies, seeded
and finely chopped
30ml/2 tbsp Thai fish sauce
5ml/1 tsp sugar
cooked rice, to serve
lime wedges, to garnish

For the sauce
90ml/6 tbsp rice vinegar
60ml/4 tbsp sugar
2.5ml/½ tsp salt
2 garlic cloves, crushed
1 small fresh red chilli, seeded and
finely chopped
115g/4oz/4 cups fresh coriander
(cilantro), finely chopped

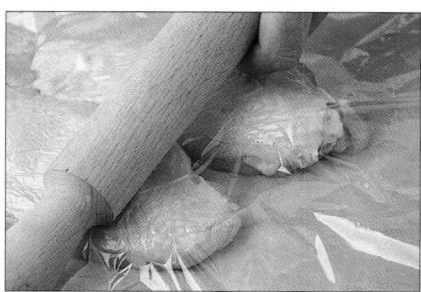

1 Lay the chicken breast portions between two sheets of clear film (plastic wrap), baking parchment or foil and beat with the side of a rolling pin or the flat side of a meat tenderizer until the meat is about half its original thickness. Place in a large, shallow dish or bowl.

2 Mix together the sesame oil, garlic, coriander roots, red chillies, fish sauce and sugar in a jug (pitcher), stirring until the sugar has dissolved. Pour the mixture over the chicken and turn to coat. Cover with clear film and set aside to marinate in a cool place for at least 20 minutes. Meanwhile, make the sauce.

3 Heat the vinegar in a small pan, add the sugar and stir until dissolved. Add the salt and stir until the mixture begins to thicken. Add the remaining sauce ingredients, stir well, then spoon the sauce into a serving bowl.

4 Preheat the grill (broiler) and cook the chicken for 5 minutes. Turn and baste with the marinade, then cook for 5 minutes more, or until cooked through and golden. Serve with rice and the sauce, garnished with lime wedges.

ROAST LIME CHICKEN
WITH SWEET POTATOES

IN THAILAND, THIS CHICKEN WOULD BE SPIT-ROASTED, AS OVENS ARE SELDOM USED. HOWEVER, IT WORKS VERY WELL AS A CONVENTIONAL ROAST. THE SWEET POTATOES ARE AN INSPIRED ADDITION.

SERVES FOUR

INGREDIENTS

    4 garlic cloves, 2 finely chopped
      and 2 bruised but left whole
    small bunch coriander (cilantro),
      with roots, coarsely chopped
    5ml/1 tsp ground turmeric
    5cm/2in piece fresh turmeric
    1 roasting chicken, about 1.5kg/3¼lb
    1 lime, cut in half
    4 medium/large sweet potatoes,
      peeled and cut into thick wedges
    300ml/½ pint/1¼ cups chicken
      or vegetable stock
    30ml/2 tbsp soy sauce
    salt and ground black pepper

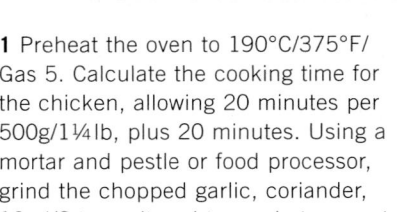

1 Preheat the oven to 190°C/375°F/ Gas 5. Calculate the cooking time for the chicken, allowing 20 minutes per 500g/1¼lb, plus 20 minutes. Using a mortar and pestle or food processor, grind the chopped garlic, coriander, 10ml/2 tsp salt and turmeric to a paste.

2 Place the chicken in a roasting pan and smear it with the paste. Squeeze the lime juice over and place the lime halves and garlic cloves in the cavity. Cover with foil and roast in the oven.

3 Meanwhile, bring a pan of water to the boil and par-boil the sweet potatoes for 10–15 minutes, until just tender. Drain well and place them around the chicken in the roasting pan. Baste with the cooking juices and sprinkle with salt and pepper. Replace the foil and return the chicken to the oven.

4 About 20 minutes before the end of cooking, remove the foil and baste the chicken. Turn the sweet potatoes over.

5 At the end of the calculated roasting time, check that the chicken is cooked. Lift it out of the roasting pan, tip it so that all the juices collected in the cavity drain into the pan, then place the bird on a carving board. Cover it with tented foil and leave it to rest before carving. Transfer the sweet potatoes to a serving dish and keep them hot in the oven while you make the gravy.

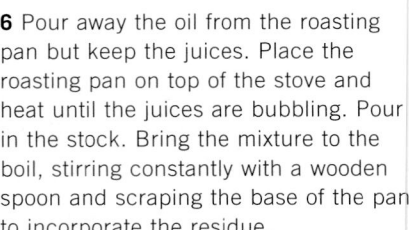

6 Pour away the oil from the roasting pan but keep the juices. Place the roasting pan on top of the stove and heat until the juices are bubbling. Pour in the stock. Bring the mixture to the boil, stirring constantly with a wooden spoon and scraping the base of the pan to incorporate the residue.

7 Stir in the soy sauce and check the seasoning before straining the gravy into a jug (pitcher). Serve it with the carved meat and the sweet potatoes.

COOK'S TIPS
• When the chicken is cooked, the legs should move freely. Insert the tip of a sharp knife or a skewer into the thickest part of one of the thighs. The juices that emerge from the cut should run clear. If there are any traces of pinkness, return the chicken to the oven for a little longer.
• Although originally native to tropical America, sweet potatoes are now a popular food crop throughout South-east Asia. There are many varieties and the flesh ranges in texture from floury to moist and in colour from deep orange through gold to white.

CHINESE DUCK CURRY

A RICHLY SPICED CURRY THAT ILLUSTRATES THE POWERFUL CHINESE INFLUENCE ON THAI CUISINE. THE DUCK IS BEST MARINATED FOR AS LONG AS POSSIBLE, ALTHOUGH IT TASTES GOOD EVEN IF YOU ONLY HAVE TIME TO MARINATE IT BRIEFLY.

SERVES FOUR

INGREDIENTS

    4 duck breast portions, skin and
      bones removed
    30ml/2 tbsp five-spice powder
    30ml/2 tbsp sesame oil
    grated rind and juice of 1 orange
    1 medium butternut squash, peeled
      and cubed
    10ml/2 tsp Thai red curry paste
    30ml/2 tbsp Thai fish sauce
    15ml/1 tbsp palm sugar or light
      muscovado (brown) sugar
    300ml/½ pint/1¼ cups coconut milk
    2 fresh red chillies, seeded
    4 kaffir lime leaves, torn
    small bunch coriander (cilantro),
      chopped, to garnish

1 Cut the duck meat into bitesize pieces and place in a bowl with the five-spice powder, sesame oil and orange rind and juice. Stir well to mix all the ingredients and coat the duck in the marinade. Cover the bowl with clear film (plastic wrap) and set aside in a cool place to marinate for at least 15 minutes.

2 Meanwhile, bring a pan of water to the boil. Add the squash and cook for 10–15 minutes, until just tender. Drain well and set aside.

3 Pour the marinade from the duck into a wok and heat until boiling. Stir in the curry paste and cook for 2–3 minutes, until well blended and fragrant. Add the duck and cook for 3–4 minutes, stirring constantly, until browned on all sides.

4 Add the fish sauce and palm sugar and cook for 2 minutes more. Stir in the coconut milk until the mixture is smooth, then add the cooked squash, with the chillies and lime leaves.

5 Simmer gently, stirring frequently, for 5 minutes, then spoon into a dish, sprinkle with the coriander and serve.

VARIATION
This dish works just as well with skinless, boneless chicken breast portions.

STIR-FRIED PORK <u>WITH</u> DRIED SHRIMP

YOU MIGHT EXPECT THE DRIED SHRIMP TO GIVE THIS DISH A FISHY FLAVOUR, BUT INSTEAD IT SIMPLY IMPARTS A DELICIOUS SAVOURY TASTE.

SERVES FOUR

INGREDIENTS

- 250g/9oz pork fillet (tenderloin), sliced
- 30ml/2 tbsp vegetable oil
- 2 garlic cloves, finely chopped
- 45ml/3 tbsp dried shrimp
- 10ml/2 tsp dried shrimp paste or 5mm/¼ in piece from block of shrimp paste
- 30ml/2 tbsp soy sauce
- juice of 1 lime
- 15ml/1 tbsp palm sugar or light muscovado (brown) sugar
- 1 small fresh red or green chilli, seeded and finely chopped
- 4 pak choi (bok choy) or 450g/1lb spring greens (collards), shredded

1 Place the pork in the freezer for about 30 minutes, until firm. Using a sharp knife, cut it into thin slices.

2 Heat the oil in a wok or frying pan and cook the garlic until golden brown. Add the pork and stir-fry for about 4 minutes, until just cooked through.

3 Add the dried shrimp, then stir in the shrimp paste, with the soy sauce, lime juice and sugar. Add the chilli and pak choi or spring greens and toss over the heat until the vegetables are just wilted.

4 Transfer the stir-fry to warm individual bowls and serve immediately.

PORK BELLY <u>WITH</u> FIVE SPICES

THE CHINESE INFLUENCE ON THAI CUISINE STEMS FROM THE EARLY YEARS OF ITS HISTORY, WHEN COLONISTS FROM SOUTHERN CHINA SETTLED IN THE COUNTRY, BRINGING WITH THEM DISHES LIKE THIS, ALTHOUGH THAI COOKS HAVE PROVIDED THEIR OWN UNIQUE IMPRINT.

SERVES FOUR

INGREDIENTS

   1 large bunch fresh coriander
    (cilantro) with roots
   30ml/2 tbsp vegetable oil
   1 garlic clove, crushed
   30ml/2 tbsp five-spice powder
   500g/1¼lb pork belly, cut into
    2.5cm/1in pieces
   400g/14oz can chopped tomatoes
   150ml/¼ pint/⅔ cup hot water
   30ml/2 tbsp dark soy sauce
   45ml/3 tbsp Thai fish sauce
   30ml/2 tbsp granulated sugar
   1 lime, halved

COOK'S TIP
Make sure that you buy Chinese five-spice powder, as the Indian variety is made up from quite different spices.

1 Cut off the coriander roots. Chop five of them finely and freeze the remainder for another occasion. Chop the coriander stalks and leaves and set them aside. Keep the roots separate.

2 Heat the oil in a large pan and cook the garlic until golden brown. Stirring constantly, add the chopped coriander roots and then the five-spice powder.

3 Add the pork and stir-fry until the meat is thoroughly coated in spices and has browned. Stir in the tomatoes and hot water. Bring to the boil, then stir in the soy sauce, fish sauce and sugar.

4 Reduce the heat, cover the pan and simmer for 30 minutes. Stir in the chopped coriander stalks and leaves, squeeze over the lime juice and serve.

PORK CHOPS WITH FIELD MUSHROOMS

IN THAILAND, MEAT IS FREQUENTLY COOKED OVER A BRAZIER OR OPEN FIRE, SO IT ISN'T SURPRISING THAT MANY TASTY BARBECUE-STYLE DISHES COME FROM THERE. THESE FABULOUS PORK CHOPS ARE GREAT FAVOURITES WITH EVERYONE AND ARE DELICIOUS SERVED WITH NOODLES OR RICE.

SERVES FOUR

INGREDIENTS
    4 pork chops
    4 large field (portabello) mushrooms
    45ml/3 tbsp vegetable oil
    4 fresh red chillies, seeded and
        thinly sliced
    45ml/3 tbsp Thai fish sauce
    90ml/6 tbsp fresh lime juice
    4 shallots, chopped
    5ml/1 tsp roasted ground rice
    30ml/2 tbsp spring onions
        (scallions), chopped, plus shredded
        spring onions to garnish
    coriander (cilantro) leaves, to garnish
For the marinade
    2 garlic cloves, chopped
    15ml/1 tbsp granulated sugar
    15ml/1 tbsp Thai fish sauce
    30ml/2 tbsp soy sauce
    15ml/1 tbsp sesame oil
    15ml/1 tbsp whisky or dry sherry
    2 lemon grass stalks, finely chopped
    2 spring onions (scallions), chopped

1 Make the marinade. Combine the garlic, sugar, sauces, oil and whisky or sherry in a large, shallow dish. Stir in the lemon grass and spring onions.

2 Add the pork chops, turning to coat them in the marinade. Cover and leave to marinate for 1–2 hours.

3 Lift the chops out of the marinade and place them on a barbecue grid over hot coals or on a grill (broiler) rack. Add the mushrooms and brush them with 15ml/1 tbsp of the oil. Cook the pork chops for 5–7 minutes on each side and the mushrooms for about 2 minutes. Brush both with the marinade while cooking.

4 Heat the remaining oil in a wok or small frying pan, then remove the pan from the heat and stir in the chillies, fish sauce, lime juice, shallots, ground rice and chopped spring onions. Put the pork chops and mushrooms on a large serving plate and spoon over the sauce. Garnish with the coriander leaves and shredded spring onion.

BEEF STEW WITH STAR ANISE

NOT A WESTERN IDEA OF A STEW, BUT MORE OF A FRAGRANT SOUP WITH TENDER MORSELS OF BEEF.
THE BEANSPROUTS, SPRING ONION AND CORIANDER ARE ADDED AT THE END OF COOKING FOR A
DELIGHTFUL CONTRAST IN TASTE AND TEXTURE.

SERVES FOUR

INGREDIENTS
1 litre/1¾ pints/4 cups vegetable or
  chicken stock
450g/1lb beef steak, cut into slivers
3 garlic cloves, finely chopped
3 coriander (cilantro) roots,
  finely chopped
2 cinnamon sticks
4 star anise
30ml/2 tbsp light soy sauce
30ml/2 tbsp Thai fish sauce
5ml/1 tsp granulated sugar
115g/4oz/1⅓ cups beansprouts
1 spring onion (scallion),
  finely chopped
small bunch fresh coriander
  (cilantro), coarsely chopped

1 Pour the stock into a large, heavy pan. Add the beef, garlic, chopped coriander roots, cinnamon sticks, star anise, soy sauce, fish sauce and sugar. Bring to the boil, then reduce the heat to low and simmer for 30 minutes. Skim off any foam that rises to the surface of the liquid with a slotted spoon.

2 Meanwhile, divide the beansprouts among four individual serving bowls. Remove and discard the cinnamon sticks and star anise from the stew with a slotted spoon. Ladle the stew over the beansprouts, garnish with the chopped spring onion and chopped fresh coriander and serve immediately.

DRY BEEF CURRY WITH PEANUT AND LIME

ORIGINATING FROM THE MOUNTAINOUS NORTHERN REGIONS OF THAILAND, DRY CURRIES ARE NOW POPULAR THROUGHOUT THE COUNTRY. THIS DRY BEEF CURRY IS USUALLY SERVED WITH A MOIST DISH SUCH AS NORTHERN FISH CURRY WITH SHALLOTS AND LEMON GRASS.

SERVES FOUR TO SIX

INGREDIENTS
400g/14oz can coconut milk
900g/2lb stewing steak,
  finely chopped
300ml/½ pint/1¼ cups beef stock
30ml/2 tbsp crunchy peanut butter
juice of 2 limes
lime slices, shredded coriander
  (cilantro) and fresh red chilli slices,
  to garnish

For the red curry paste
30ml/2 tbsp coriander seeds
5ml/1 tsp cumin seeds
seeds from 6 green cardamom pods
2.5ml/½ tsp grated or ground nutmeg
1.5ml/¼ tsp ground cloves
2.5ml/½ tsp ground cinnamon
20ml/4 tsp paprika
pared rind of 1 mandarin orange,
  finely chopped
4–5 small fresh red chillies, seeded
  and finely chopped
25ml/5 tsp granulated sugar
2.5ml/½ tsp salt
1 piece lemon grass, about 10cm/4in
  long, shredded
3 garlic cloves, crushed
2cm/¾in piece fresh galangal,
  peeled and finely chopped
4 red shallots, finely chopped
1 piece shrimp paste,
  2cm/¾in square
50g/2oz coriander (cilantro) root or
  stem, chopped
juice of ½ lime
30ml/2 tbsp vegetable oil

1 Strain the coconut milk into a bowl, retaining the thicker coconut milk in the strainer or sieve.

2 Pour the thin coconut milk from the bowl into a large, heavy pan, then scrape in half the residue from the sieve. Reserve the remaining thick coconut milk. Add the chopped steak. Pour in the beef stock and bring to the boil. Reduce the heat, cover the pan and simmer gently for 50 minutes.

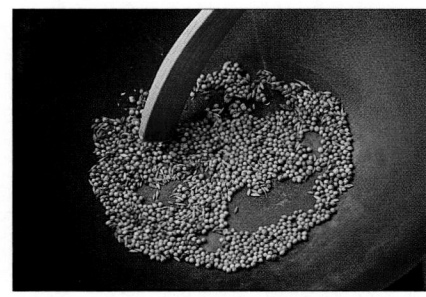

3 Make the curry paste. Dry-fry all the seeds for 1–2 minutes. Tip into a bowl and add the nutmeg, cloves, cinnamon, paprika and orange rind. Pound the chillies with the sugar and salt. Add the spice mixture, lemon grass, garlic, galangal, shallots and shrimp paste and pound to a paste. Work in the coriander, lime juice and oil.

4 Strain the beef, reserving the cooking liquid, and place a cupful of liquid in a wok. Stir in 30–45ml/2–3 tbsp of the curry paste, according to taste. Boil rapidly until all the liquid has evaporated. Stir in the reserved thick coconut milk, the peanut butter and the beef. Simmer, uncovered, for 15–20 minutes, adding a little more cooking liquid if the mixture starts to stick to the pan, but keep the curry dry.

5 Just before serving, stir in the lime juice. Serve in warmed bowls, garnished with the lime slices, shredded coriander and sliced red chillies.

VARIATION
The curry is equally delicious made with lean leg or shoulder of lamb.

RICE AND NOODLES

Thailand is one of the world's major producers of both long grain and glutinous rice. Thai fragrant rice, also known as jasmine rice, is valued for its subtle fragrance. It goes well with both savoury and sweet dishes and is delicious when cooked in coconut milk. Noodles are also popular throughout Thailand. Most of the noodles on sale are made from rice, although you will also find mung bean noodles, whose almost glassy appearance makes them a good choice for stir-fries.

CURRIED CHICKEN AND RICE

THIS SIMPLE ONE-POT MEAL IS PERFECT FOR CASUAL ENTERTAINING. IT CAN BE MADE USING VIRTUALLY ANY MEAT OR VEGETABLES THAT YOU HAVE TO HAND.

SERVES FOUR

INGREDIENTS

  60ml/4 tbsp vegetable oil
  4 garlic cloves, finely chopped
  1 chicken (about 1.5kg/3–3½ lb)
    or chicken pieces, skin and bones
    removed and meat cut into
    bitesize pieces
  5ml/1 tsp garam masala
  450g/1lb/2⅔ cups jasmine rice,
    rinsed and drained
  10ml/2 tsp salt
  1 litre/1¾ pints/4 cups
    chicken stock
  small bunch fresh coriander
    (cilantro), chopped, to garnish

COOK'S TIP
You will probably need to brown the chicken in batches, so don't be tempted to add too much chicken at once.

1 Heat the oil in a wok or flameproof casserole, which has a lid. Add the garlic and cook over a low to medium heat until golden brown. Add the chicken, increase the heat and brown the pieces on all sides (see Cook's Tip).

2 Add the garam masala, stir well to coat the chicken all over in the spice, then tip in the drained rice. Add the salt and stir to mix.

3 Pour in the stock, stir well, then cover the wok or casserole and bring to the boil. Reduce the heat to low and simmer gently for 10 minutes, until the rice is cooked and tender.

4 Lift the wok or casserole off the heat, leaving the lid on, and leave for 10 minutes. Fluff up the rice grains with a fork and spoon on to a platter. Sprinkle with the coriander and serve immediately.

THAI FRIED RICE

THIS SUBSTANTIAL AND TASTY DISH IS BASED ON JASMINE RICE. DICED CHICKEN, RED PEPPER AND CORN KERNELS ADD COLOUR AND EXTRA FLAVOUR.

SERVES FOUR

INGREDIENTS
  475ml/16fl oz/2 cups water
  50g/2oz/½ cup coconut milk powder
  350g/12oz/1¾ cups jasmine
    rice, rinsed
  30ml/2 tbsp groundnut (peanut) oil
  2 garlic cloves, chopped
  1 small onion, finely chopped
  2.5cm/1in piece of fresh root ginger,
    peeled and grated
  225g/8oz skinless, boneless chicken
    breast portions, cut into
    1cm/½in dice
  1 red (bell) pepper, seeded
    and sliced
  115g/4oz/1 cup drained canned
    whole kernel corn
  5ml/1 tsp chilli oil
  5ml/1 tsp hot curry powder
  2 eggs, beaten
  salt
  spring onion (scallion) shreds,
    to garnish

1 Pour the water into a pan and whisk in the coconut milk powder. Add the rice and bring to the boil. Reduce the heat, cover and cook for 12 minutes, or until the rice is tender and the liquid has been absorbed. Spread the rice on a baking sheet and leave until cold.

2 Heat the oil in a wok, add the garlic, onion and ginger and stir-fry over a medium heat for 2 minutes.

COOK'S TIP
It is important that the rice is completely cold before being fried.

3 Push the onion mixture to the sides of the wok, add the chicken to the centre and stir-fry for 2 minutes. Add the rice and toss well. Stir-fry over a high heat for about 3 minutes more, until the chicken is cooked through.

4 Stir in the sliced red pepper, corn, chilli oil and curry powder, with salt to taste. Toss over the heat for 1 minute. Stir in the beaten eggs and cook for 1 minute more. Garnish with the spring onion shreds and serve.

FESTIVE RICE

THIS PRETTY DISH IS TRADITIONALLY SHAPED INTO A CONE AND SURROUNDED BY A VARIETY OF ACCOMPANIMENTS BEFORE BEING SERVED.

2 Heat the oil in a frying pan with a lid. Cook the garlic, onions and turmeric over a low heat for 2–3 minutes, until the onions have softened. Add the rice and stir well to coat in oil.

3 Pour in the water and coconut milk and add the lemon grass. Bring to the boil, stirring. Cover the pan and cook gently for 12 minutes, or until all the liquid has been absorbed by the rice.

SERVES EIGHT

INGREDIENTS
 450g/1lb/2⅔ cups jasmine rice
 60ml/4 tbsp oil
 2 garlic cloves, crushed
 2 onions, thinly sliced
 2.5ml/½ tsp ground turmeric
 750ml/1¼ pints/3 cups water
 400ml/14fl oz can coconut milk
 1–2 lemon grass stalks, bruised
For the accompaniments
 omelette strips
 2 fresh red chillies, seeded
 and shredded
 cucumber chunks
 tomato wedges
 deep-fried onions
 prawn (shrimp) crackers

1 Put the jasmine rice in a large sieve (strainer) and rinse it thoroughly under cold water. Drain well.

COOK'S TIP
Jasmine rice is widely available in most supermarkets and Asian stores. It is also known as Thai fragrant rice.

4 Remove the pan from the heat and lift the lid. Cover with a clean dishtowel, replace the lid and leave to stand in a warm place for 15 minutes. Remove the lemon grass, mound the rice mixture in a cone on a serving platter and garnish with the accompaniments, then serve.

SAVOURY FRIED RICE

THIS IS TYPICAL THAI STREET FOOD, EATEN AT ALL TIMES OF THE DAY. THE RECIPE CAN BE ADAPTED TO USE WHATEVER VEGETABLES YOU HAVE AVAILABLE AND YOU COULD ALSO ADD MEAT OR SHELLFISH.

SERVES TWO

INGREDIENTS
30ml/2 tbsp vegetable oil
2 garlic cloves, finely chopped
1 small fresh red chilli, seeded and finely chopped
50g/2oz/½ cup cashew nuts, toasted
50g/2oz/⅔ cup desiccated (dry unsweetened shredded) coconut, toasted
2.5ml/½ tsp palm sugar or light muscovado (brown) sugar
30ml/2 tbsp light soy sauce
15ml/1 tbsp rice vinegar
1 egg
115g/4oz/1 cup green beans, sliced
½ spring cabbage or 115g/4oz spring greens (collards) or pak choi (bok choy), shredded
90g/3½oz jasmine rice, cooked
lime wedges, to serve

1 Heat the oil in a wok or large, heavy frying pan. Add the garlic and cook over a medium to high heat until golden. Do not let it burn or it will taste bitter.

2 Add the red chilli, cashew nuts and toasted coconut to the wok or pan and stir-fry briefly, taking care to prevent the coconut from scorching. Stir in the sugar, soy sauce and rice vinegar. Toss over the heat for 1–2 minutes.

3 Push the stir-fry to one side of the wok or pan and break the egg into the empty side. When the egg is almost set stir it into the garlic and chilli mixture with a wooden spatula or spoon.

4 Add the green beans, greens and cooked rice. Stir over the heat until the greens have just wilted, then spoon into a dish to serve. Offer the lime wedges separately, for squeezing over the rice.

THAI FRIED NOODLES

PHAT THAI HAS A FASCINATING FLAVOUR AND TEXTURE. IT IS MADE WITH RICE NOODLES AND IS CONSIDERED ONE OF THE NATIONAL DISHES OF THAILAND.

SERVES FOUR TO SIX

INGREDIENTS
16 raw tiger prawns
   (jumbo shrimp)
350g/12oz rice noodles
45ml/3 tbsp vegetable oil
15ml/1 tbsp chopped garlic
2 eggs, lightly beaten
15ml/1 tbsp dried
   shrimp, rinsed
30ml/2 tbsp pickled
   mooli (daikon)
50g/2oz fried tofu, cut into
   small slivers
2.5ml/½ tsp dried chilli flakes
1 large bunch garlic chives,
   about 115g/4oz, cut into
   5cm/2in lengths
225g/8oz/2½ cups beansprouts
50g/2oz/½ cup roasted peanuts,
   coarsely ground
5ml/1 tsp granulated sugar
15ml/1 tbsp dark soy sauce
30ml/2 tbsp Thai fish sauce
30ml/2 tbsp tamarind juice, made
   by mixing tamarind paste with
   warm water
To garnish
   fresh coriander (cilantro) leaves
   lime wedges

1 Peel the prawns, leaving the tails intact. Carefully cut along the back of each prawn and remove the dark vein.

2 Place the rice noodles in a large bowl, add warm water to cover and leave to soak for 20–30 minutes, then drain thoroughly and set aside.

3 Heat 15ml/1 tbsp of the oil in a wok. Stir-fry the garlic until golden. Stir in the prawns and cook for 1–2 minutes, until pink. Remove and set aside.

4 Heat 15ml/1 tbsp of the remaining oil in the wok. Add the eggs and tilt the wok to make a thin layer. Stir to scramble and break up. Remove from the wok and set aside with the prawns.

5 Heat the remaining oil in the same wok. Add the dried shrimp, pickled mooli, tofu slivers and dried chilli flakes. Stir briefly. Add the noodles and stir-fry for about 5 minutes.

6 Add the garlic chives, half the beansprouts and half the peanuts. Add the granulated sugar, then season with soy sauce, fish sauce and tamarind juice. Mix well and cook until the noodles are heated through.

7 Return the prawn and egg mixture to the wok and mix with the noodles. Serve topped with the remaining beansprouts and peanuts, and garnished with the coriander leaves and lime wedges.

COOK'S TIP
There are numerous species of prawns (shrimp) and they range in colour from black to white, although most turn pink when cooked. Genuine Indo-Pacific tiger prawns, of which there are several types, have a fine flavour and a good texture. They grow up to 28cm/11in in length. However, not all large, warm water varieties are so succulent, and even farmed prawns tend to be quite expensive.

SPECIAL CHOW MEIN

ANOTHER EXAMPLE OF THE CHINESE INFLUENCE IN THAI COOKING. LAP CHEONG IS A SPECIAL AIR-DRIED CHINESE SAUSAGE AND IS AVAILABLE FROM MOST CHINESE SUPERMARKETS.

SERVES FOUR TO SIX

INGREDIENTS
    450g/1lb egg noodles
    45ml/3 tbsp vegetable oil
    2 garlic cloves, sliced
    5ml/1 tsp chopped fresh root ginger
    2 fresh red chillies, seeded
      and chopped
    2 lap cheong, total weight
      about 75g/3oz, rinsed and
      sliced (optional)
    1 skinless, boneless chicken breast
      portion, thinly sliced
    16 uncooked tiger prawns (jumbo
      shrimp), peeled, tails left intact,
      and deveined
    115g/4oz/2 cups green beans
    225g/8oz/2½ cups beansprouts
    small bunch garlic chives,
      about 50g/2oz
    30ml/2 tbsp soy sauce
    15ml/1 tbsp oyster sauce
    15ml/1 tbsp sesame oil
    salt and ground black pepper
    2 shredded spring onions (scallions)
      and fresh coriander (cilantro)
      leaves, to garnish

1 Cook the noodles in a large pan of boiling water, according to the instructions on the packet. Drain well.

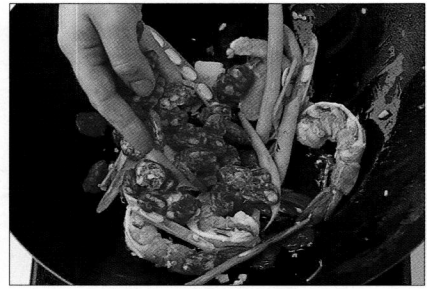

2 Heat 15ml/1 tbsp of the oil in a wok or large frying pan and stir-fry the garlic, ginger and chillies for 2 minutes. Add the lap cheong, if using, chicken, prawns and beans. Stir-fry over a high heat for 2 minutes more, or until the chicken and prawns are cooked. Transfer the mixture to a bowl and set aside.

3 Heat the rest of the oil in the wok. Add the beansprouts and garlic chives and stir-fry for 1–2 minutes.

4 Add the drained noodles and toss over the heat to mix. Season with the soy sauce, oyster sauce and salt and pepper to taste. Return the prawn mixture to the wok. Mix well with the noodles and toss until heated through.

5 Stir the sesame oil into the noodles. Spoon into a warmed bowl and serve immediately, garnished with the spring onions and coriander leaves.

THAI CRISPY NOODLES <u>WITH</u> BEEF

RICE VERMICELLI IS DEEP-FRIED BEFORE BEING ADDED TO THIS DISH, AND IN THE PROCESS THE VERMICELLI EXPANDS TO AT LEAST FOUR TIMES ITS ORIGINAL SIZE.

SERVES FOUR

INGREDIENTS
   450g/1lb rump (round) steak
   teriyaki sauce, for brushing
   175g/6oz rice vermicelli
   groundnut (peanut) oil, for deep-
      frying and stir-frying
   8 spring onions (scallions),
      diagonally sliced
   2 garlic cloves, crushed
   4–5 carrots, cut into julienne strips
   1–2 fresh red chillies, seeded and
      finely sliced
   2 small courgettes (zucchini),
      diagonally sliced
   5ml/1 tsp grated fresh root ginger
   60ml/4 tbsp rice vinegar
   90ml/6 tbsp light soy sauce
   about 475ml/16fl oz/2 cups
      spicy stock

1 Beat the steak to about 2.5cm/1in thick. Place in a shallow dish, brush generously with the teriyaki sauce and set aside for 2–4 hours to marinate.

2 Separate the rice vermicelli into manageable loops. Pour oil into a large wok to a depth of about 5cm/2in, and heat until a strand of vermicelli cooks as soon as it is lowered into the oil.

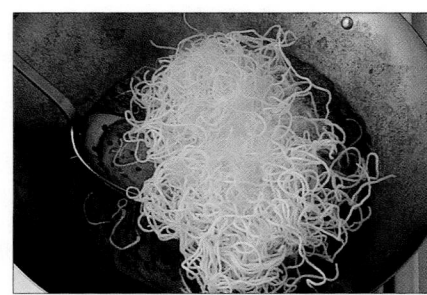

3 Carefully add a loop of vermicelli to the oil. Almost immediately, turn to cook on the other side, then remove and drain on kitchen paper. Repeat with the remaining loops. Transfer the cooked noodles to a separate wok or deep serving bowl and keep them warm while you cook the steak and vegetables.

4 Strain the oil from the wok into a heatproof bowl and set it aside. Heat 15ml/1 tbsp groundnut oil in the clean wok. When it sizzles, fry the steak for about 30 seconds on each side, until browned. Transfer to a board and cut into thick slices. The meat should be well browned on the outside but still pink inside. Set aside.

5 Add a little extra oil to the wok, add the spring onions, garlic and carrots and stir-fry over a medium heat for 5–6 minutes, until the carrots are slightly soft and have a glazed appearance. Add the chillies, courgettes and ginger and stir-fry for 1–2 minutes.

6 Stir in the rice vinegar, soy sauce and stock. Cook for 4 minutes, or until the sauce has thickened slightly. Return the slices of steak to the wok and cook for a further 1–2 minutes.

7 Spoon the steak, vegetables and sauce over the noodles and toss lightly and carefully to mix. Serve immediately.

COOK'S TIP
As soon as you add the meat mixture to the noodles, they will begin to soften in the sauce. If you wish to keep a few crispy noodles, leave some on the surface so that they do not come into contact with the hot liquid.

MEE KROB

THE NAME OF THIS DISH MEANS "DEEP-FRIED NOODLES" AND IT IS VERY POPULAR IN THAILAND. THE TASTE IS A STUNNING COMBINATION OF SWEET AND HOT, SALTY AND SOUR, WHILE THE TEXTURE CONTRIVES TO BE BOTH CRISP AND CHEWY. TO SOME WESTERN PALATES, IT MAY SEEM RATHER UNUSUAL, BUT THIS DELICIOUS DISH IS WELL WORTH MAKING.

SERVES ONE

INGREDIENTS

vegetable oil, for deep-frying
130g/4½oz rice vermicelli noodles

For the sauce
30ml/2 tbsp vegetable oil
130g/4½oz fried tofu, cut into thin strips
2 garlic cloves, finely chopped
2 small shallots, finely chopped
15ml/1 tbsp light soy sauce
30ml/2 tbsp palm sugar or light muscovado (brown) sugar
60ml/4 tbsp vegetable stock
juice of 1 lime
2.5ml/½ tsp dried chilli flakes

For the garnish
15ml/1 tbsp vegetable oil
1 egg, lightly beaten with 15ml/1 tbsp cold water
25g/1oz/⅓ cup beansprouts
1 spring onion (scallion), thinly shredded
1 fresh red chilli, seeded and finely chopped
1 whole head pickled garlic, sliced across the bulb so each slice looks like a flower

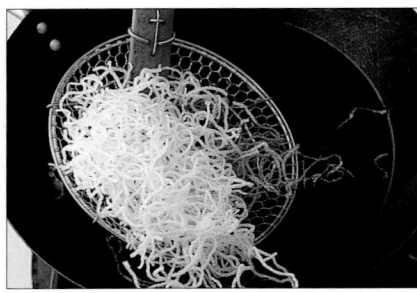

1 Heat the oil for deep-frying in a wok or large pan to 190°C/375°F or until a cube of bread, added to the oil, browns in about 45 seconds. Add the noodles and deep-fry until golden and crisp. Drain on kitchen paper and set aside.

2 Make the sauce. Heat the oil in a wok, add the fried tofu and cook over a medium heat until crisp. Using a slotted spoon, transfer it to a plate.

3 Add the garlic and shallots to the wok and cook until golden brown. Stir in the soy sauce, sugar, stock, lime juice and chilli flakes. Cook, stirring, until the mixture begins to caramelize.

4 Add the reserved tofu and stir until it has soaked up some of the liquid. Remove the wok from the heat and set aside.

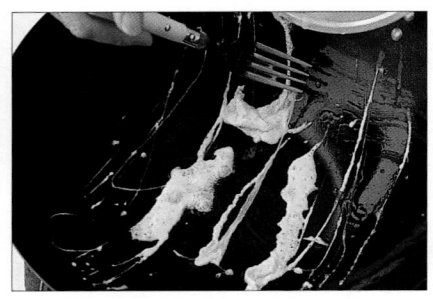

5 Prepare the egg garnish. Heat the oil in a wok or frying pan. Pour in the egg in a thin stream to form trails. As soon as it sets, lift it out with a fish slice or metal spatula and place on a plate.

6 Crumble the noodles into the tofu sauce, mix well, then spoon into warmed serving bowls. Sprinkle with the beansprouts, spring onion, fried egg strips, chilli and pickled garlic "flowers" and serve immediately.

COOK'S TIP

Successful deep-frying depends, to a large extent, on the type of oil used and the temperature to which it is heated. A bland-tasting oil, such as sunflower, will not alter the flavour of the food. All fats have a "smoke point" – the temperature at which they begin to decompose. Most vegetable oils have a high smoke point, with groundnut (peanut) oil the highest of all and so also the safest.

DESSERTS

After a spicy Thai meal, it is customary to serve a platter of fresh fruits, often carved into the most beautiful shapes, to cleanse the palate. Ices are popular too, especially when based on watermelon or coconut, while tapioca and rice puddings are more subtly flavoured than the Western versions. However, Thais also love sticky sweetmeats, and will often pick up their favourite treats at a night market, where they will be presented prettily on palm leaves or with a decoration of tiny flowers.

TAPIOCA PUDDING

THIS PUDDING, MADE FROM LARGE PEARL TAPIOCA AND COCONUT MILK AND SERVED WARM, IS MUCH LIGHTER THAN THE WESTERN-STYLE VERSION. YOU CAN ADJUST THE SWEETNESS TO YOUR TASTE. SERVE WITH LYCHEES OR THE SMALLER, SIMILAR-TASTING LONGANS — ALSO KNOWN AS "DRAGON'S EYES".

SERVES FOUR

INGREDIENTS

 115g/4oz/⅔ cup tapioca
 475ml/16fl oz/2 cups water
 175g/6oz/¾ cup granulated sugar
 pinch of salt
 250ml/8fl oz/1 cup coconut milk
 250g/9oz prepared tropical fruits
 finely shredded lime rind
  and shaved fresh coconut (optional),
  to decorate

1 Put the tapioca in a bowl and pour over warm water to cover. Leave to soak for 1 hour so the grains swell. Drain.

2 Pour the measured water in a large pan and bring to the boil over a medium heat. Add the sugar and salt and stir until dissolved.

3 Add the tapioca and coconut milk, reduce the heat to low and simmer gently for 10 minutes, or until the tapioca becomes transparent.

4 Spoon into one large or four individual bowls and serve warm with the tropical fruits. Decorate with the lime rind and coconut shavings, if using.

BAKED RICE PUDDING, THAI-STYLE

BLACK GLUTINOUS RICE, ALSO KNOWN AS BLACK STICKY RICE, HAS LONG DARK GRAINS AND A NUTTY TASTE REMINISCENT OF WILD RICE. THIS BAKED PUDDING HAS A DISTINCT CHARACTER AND FLAVOUR ALL OF ITS OWN, AS WELL AS AN INTRIGUING APPEARANCE.

SERVES FOUR TO SIX

INGREDIENTS
    175g/6oz/1 cup white or black
      glutinous rice
    30ml/2 tbsp soft light brown sugar
    475ml/16fl oz/2 cups coconut milk
    250ml/8fl oz/1 cup water
    3 eggs
    30ml/2 tbsp granulated sugar

1 Combine the glutinous rice and brown sugar in a pan. Pour in half the coconut milk and the water.

2 Bring to the boil, reduce the heat to low and simmer, stirring occasionally, for 15–20 minutes, or until the rice has absorbed most of the liquid. Preheat the oven to 150°C/300°F/Gas 2.

3 Spoon the rice mixture into a single large ovenproof dish or divide it among individual ramekins. Beat the eggs with the remaining coconut milk and sugar in a bowl.

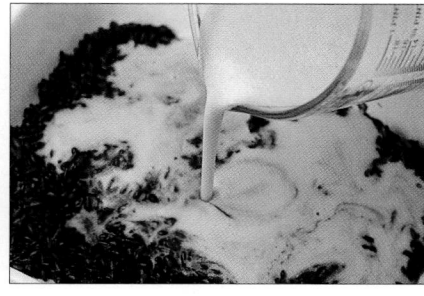

4 Strain the egg mixture into a jug (pitcher), then pour it evenly over the par-cooked rice in the dish or ramekins.

5 Place the dish or ramekins in a roasting pan. Carefully pour in enough hot water to come halfway up the sides of the dish or ramekins.

6 Cover with foil and bake for about 35–60 minutes, or until the custard has set. Serve warm or cold.

COOK'S TIP
Throughout South-east Asia, black glutinous rice is usually used for sweet dishes, while its white counterpart is more often used in savoury recipes.

STEWED PUMPKIN IN COCONUT CREAM

FRUIT STEWED IN COCONUT MILK IS A POPULAR DESSERT IN THAILAND. PUMPKINS, BANANAS AND MELONS CAN ALL BE PREPARED IN THIS SIMPLE BUT TASTY WAY.

SERVES FOUR TO SIX

INGREDIENTS
 1kg/2¼lb kabocha pumpkin
 750ml/1¼ pints/3 cups coconut milk
 175g/6oz/¾ cup granulated sugar
 pinch of salt
 4–6 fresh mint sprigs, to decorate

COOK'S TIP
To make the decoration, wash the pumpkin seeds to remove any fibres, then pat them dry on kitchen paper. Roast them in a dry frying pan, or spread them out on a baking sheet and grill (broil) until golden brown, tossing them frequently to prevent them from burning.

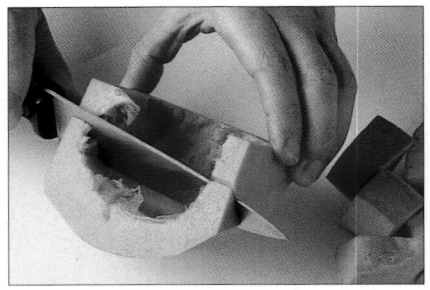

1 Cut the pumpkin in half using a large, sharp knife, then cut away and discard the skin. Scoop out the seed cluster. Reserve a few seeds and throw away the rest. Using a sharp knife, cut the pumpkin flesh into pieces that are about 5cm/2in long and 2cm/¾in thick.

2 Pour the coconut milk into a pan. Add the sugar and salt and bring to the boil. Add the pumpkin and simmer for about 10–15 minutes, until it is tender. Serve warm, in individual dishes. Decorate each serving with a mint sprig and toasted pumpkin seeds (see Cook's Tip).

MANGOES WITH STICKY RICE

STICKY RICE IS JUST AS GOOD IN DESSERTS AS IN SAVOURY DISHES, AND MANGOES, WITH THEIR DELICATE FRAGRANCE AND VELVETY FLESH, COMPLEMENT IT ESPECIALLY WELL. YOU NEED TO START PREPARING THIS DISH THE DAY BEFORE YOU INTEND TO SERVE IT.

SERVES FOUR

INGREDIENTS
 115g/4oz/⅔ cup white
  glutinous rice
 175ml/6fl oz/¾ cup thick
  coconut milk
 45ml/3 tbsp granulated sugar
 pinch of salt
 2 ripe mangoes
 strips of pared lime rind,
  to decorate

1 Rinse the glutinous rice thoroughly in several changes of cold water, then leave to soak overnight in a bowl of fresh cold water.

COOK'S TIP
Like cream, the thickest and richest part of coconut milk always rises to the top. Whenever you open a can or carton, spoon off this top layer and use it with fruit or to enrich a spicy savoury dish just before serving.

2 Drain the rice well and spread it out evenly in a steamer lined with muslin or cheesecloth. Cover and steam over a pan of simmering water for about 20 minutes, or until the rice is tender.

3 Reserve 45ml/3 tbsp of the cream from the top of the coconut milk. Pour the remainder into a pan and add the sugar and salt. Heat, stirring constantly, until the sugar has dissolved, then bring to the boil. Remove the pan from the heat, pour the coconut milk into a bowl and leave to cool.

4 Transfer the cooked rice to a bowl and pour over the cooled coconut milk mixture. Stir well, then leave the rice mixture to stand for 10–15 minutes.

5 Meanwhile, peel the mangoes, cut the flesh away from the central stones (pits) and cut into slices.

6 Spoon the rice on to individual serving plates. Arrange the mango slices on one side, then drizzle with the reserved coconut cream. Decorate with strips of lime rind and serve.

COCONUT CUSTARD

THIS TRADITIONAL DESSERT CAN BE BAKED OR STEAMED AND IS OFTEN SERVED WITH SWEET STICKY RICE AND A SELECTION OF FRESH FRUIT. MANGOES AND TAMARILLOS GO PARTICULARLY WELL WITH THE CUSTARD AND RICE.

2 Strain the mixture into a jug (pitcher), then pour it into four individual heatproof glasses, ramekins or an ovenproof dish.

3 Stand the glasses, ramekins or dish in a roasting pan. Fill the pan with hot water to reach halfway up the sides of the ramekins or dish.

4 Bake for about 35–40 minutes, or until the custards are set. Test with a fine skewer or cocktail stick (toothpick).

5 Remove the roasting pan from the oven, lift out the ramekins or dish and leave to cool.

6 If you like, turn out the custards on to serving plate(s). Decorate with the mint leaves and a dusting of icing sugar, and serve with sliced fruit.

SERVES FOUR

INGREDIENTS
  4 eggs
  75g/3oz/6 tbsp soft light brown sugar
  250ml/8fl oz/1 cup coconut milk
  5ml/1 tsp vanilla, rose or
    jasmine extract
  fresh mint leaves and icing
    (confectioners') sugar, to decorate
  sliced fruit, to serve

1 Preheat the oven to 150°C/300°F/ Gas 2. Whisk the eggs and sugar in a bowl until smooth. Add the coconut milk and extract and whisk well.

COCONUT CREAM DIAMONDS

DESSERTS LIKE THESE ARE SERVED IN COUNTRIES ALL OVER THE FAR EAST, OFTEN WITH MANGOES, PINEAPPLE OR GUAVAS. ALTHOUGH COMMERCIALLY GROUND RICE CAN BE USED FOR THIS DISH, GRINDING JASMINE RICE YOURSELF — IN A FOOD PROCESSOR — GIVES A MUCH BETTER RESULT.

SERVES FOUR TO SIX

INGREDIENTS
　　75g/3oz/scant ½ cup jasmine rice,
　　　soaked overnight in 175ml/6fl oz/
　　　¾ cup water
　　350ml/12fl oz/1½ cups
　　　coconut milk
　　150ml/¼ pint/⅔ cup single
　　　(light) cream
　　50g/2oz/¼ cup caster
　　　(superfine) sugar
　　raspberries and fresh mint leaves,
　　　to decorate
For the coulis
　　75g/3oz/¾ cup blackcurrants,
　　　stalks removed
　　30ml/2 tbsp caster (superfine) sugar
　　75g/3oz/½ cup fresh or
　　　frozen raspberries

1 Put the rice and its soaking water into a food processor and process for a few minutes until the mixture is soupy.

2 Heat the coconut milk and cream in a non-stick pan. When the mixture is on the point of boiling, stir in the rice mixture. Cook over a very gentle heat for 10 minutes, stirring constantly.

3 Stir the sugar into the coconut rice mixture and continue cooking for a further 10–15 minutes, or until the mixture is thick and creamy.

VARIATION
You could use other soft fruit in the coulis, such as blackberries or redcurrants.

4 Line a rectangular tin (pan) with non-stick baking parchment. Pour the coconut rice mixture into the tin, cool, then chill in the refrigerator until the dessert is set and firm.

5 Meanwhile, make the coulis. Put the blackcurrants in a bowl and sprinkle with the sugar. Set aside for about 30 minutes. Tip the blackcurrants and raspberries into a wire sieve set over a bowl. Using a spoon, press the fruit against the sides of the sieve so that the juices collect in the bowl. Taste the coulis and add more sugar if necessary.

6 Carefully cut the coconut cream into diamonds. Spoon a little of the coulis on to each dessert plate, arrange the coconut cream diamonds on top and decorate with the fresh raspberries and mint leaves. Serve immediately.

WATERMELON ICE

AFTER A HOT AND SPICY THAI MEAL, THE ONLY THING MORE REFRESHING THAN ICE-COLD WATERMELON IS THIS WATERMELON ICE. MAKING IT IS SIMPLICITY ITSELF.

3 Spoon the watermelon into a food processor. Process to a slush, then mix with the sugar syrup. Chill the mixture in the refrigerator for 3–4 hours.

4 Strain the mixture into a freezerproof container. Freeze for 2 hours, then remove from the freezer and beat with a fork to break up the ice crystals. Return the mixture to the freezer and freeze for 3 hours more, beating the mixture at half-hourly intervals. Freeze until firm.

5 Alternatively, use an ice cream maker. Pour the chilled mixture into the machine and churn until it is firm enough to scoop. Serve immediately, or scrape into a freezerproof container and store in the freezer.

6 About 30 minutes before serving, transfer the ice to the refrigerator so that it softens slightly. This allows the full flavour of the watermelon to be enjoyed and makes it easier to scoop.

SERVES FOUR TO SIX

INGREDIENTS
90ml/6 tbsp caster
  (superfine) sugar
105ml/7 tbsp water
4 kaffir lime leaves, torn into
  small pieces
500g/1¼lb watermelon

1 Put the sugar, water and lime leaves in a pan. Heat gently until the sugar has dissolved. Pour into a large bowl and set aside to cool.

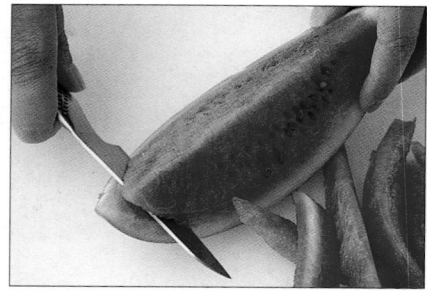

2 Cut the watermelon into wedges with a large knife. Cut the flesh from the rind, remove the seeds and chop.

COCONUT AND LEMON GRASS ICE CREAM

THE COMBINATION OF CREAM AND COCONUT MILK MAKES FOR A WONDERFULLY RICH ICE CREAM.
THE LEMON GRASS FLAVOURING IS VERY SUBTLE, BUT QUITE DELICIOUS.

SERVES FOUR

INGREDIENTS

2 lemon grass stalks
475ml/16fl oz/2 cups double
  (heavy) cream
120ml/4fl oz/½ cup coconut milk
4 large (US extra large) eggs
105ml/7 tbsp caster
  (superfine) sugar
5ml/1 tsp vanilla essence (extract)

1 Cut the lemon grass stalks in half lengthways. Use a mallet or rolling pin to mash the pieces, breaking up the fibres so that all the flavour is released.

2 Pour the cream and coconut milk into a pan. Add the lemon grass stalks and heat gently, stirring frequently, until the mixture starts to simmer.

3 Put the eggs, sugar and vanilla essence in a large bowl. Using an electric whisk, whisk until the mixture is very light and fluffy.

4 Strain the cream mixture into a heatproof bowl that will fit over a pan of simmering water. Whisk in the egg mixture, then place the bowl over the pan and continue to whisk until the mixture thickens. Remove it from the heat and leave to cool. Chill the coconut custard in the refrigerator for 3–4 hours.

5 Pour the mixture into a plastic tub or similar freezerproof container. Freeze for 4 hours, beating two or three times at hourly intervals with a fork to break up the ice crystals.

6 Alternatively, use an ice cream maker. Pour the chilled mixture into the machine and churn until it is firm enough to scoop. Serve immediately, or scrape into a freezerproof container and place in the freezer.

7 About 30 minutes before serving, transfer the container to the refrigerator so that the ice cream softens slightly. Serve in scoops.

VARIATION
To make Coconut and Mango Ice Cream, purée the contents of two 400g/14oz cans of mangoes in syrup and add to the coconut custard before chilling it in the refrigerator. An ice cream made in this way will serve six.

INDEX